THROUGH A PARADOX LENS

Published by Wisdom Mates Press
Niantic CT USA
Wisdommatespress.com
Cover design by Haacker Communications

Library of Congress Control Number: 2023905483

ISBN 979-8-218-17085-1 (Paperback)
ISBN 979-8-218-17086-8 (E-Book)

First Printing, 2023

Through A Paradox Lens

An Introduction to Paradoxical Thinking and Problem Solving

JEFF FLESHER PHD

Wisdom Mates Press

Contents

Acknowledgements

The Paradoxical Awareness model below describes my appreciation for those who have contributed to my understanding and application of paradoxical thinking and problem solving. A few of them are listed by name. They are the tip of the iceberg of a very long list.

Acknowledgements
Influencers And Supporters

Family And Friends
Teachers And Students
Playmates And Colleagues
Researchers And Practitioners
Experience And Reflection
Sacred And Profane
Ancient And Modern

Appreciation And Contribution

Thank You

The Tip of the Iceberg

Bonnie Flesher, Keith Williams, Patrick Boyle, Peggy Taylor, Debra Bragg, Helen Haacker, Robert Pease, Philip Anderson, Jake Jacobs, Bill Putsis, Carol Younes, Carlos Correia, Greg Kane, Scott Johnson, Norma Scagnoli, Kaley Poll, Sarah Myers, David Hulin, James Flesher, and Rhonda Harrison.

Introduction

Under heaven all can see beauty as beauty,
only because there is ugliness.

All can know good as good only because there is evil.
Being and nonbeing produce each other.

The difficult is born in the easy.
Long is defined by short, the high by the low.

Before and after go along with each other.

So the sage lives openly with apparent duality
and paradoxical unity.

Tao Te Ching (Interpretation Dyer, 2007)

In the verses from the Tao, we are introduced to a paradoxical interpretation of reality. We see the world as what it is and what it is not. We learn by discovering difference and nuance and we are guided by our subsequent judgements of what we think is good and bad. We also learn that a wise person navigates the world of seeming difference and maintains awareness of the whole, with harmonized dual perspectives of the whole (Unity) and its contributing parts (Paradoxes).

The purpose of this book is to increase your paradoxical awareness and provide you some tools and approaches to find practical utility in understanding and problem solving through a paradox lens. For our purposes we will define paradox broadly as situationally relevant aspects of context, observed characteristics, perspectives, and sensemaking tools. Paradox is a phenomenon that describes connections, boundaries, peculiarities, wisdom and meaning. They also describe all kinds of conflicts from challenging conditions to multiple good choices and seemingly impossible situations.

Paradoxes are not hard to find. They are ubiquitous and sometimes you need to look. Sometimes they are gestalts that leap into our consciousness or gently emerge as new meaning in a familiar place. I find these realizations exhilarating, fun, and affirming like revelations given to me. They are not inherently good or bad, and yet they can help us to understand what good and bad are for us in certain contexts or relationships. When I first started to work directly with these in organizational problem solving it was to help people see Both/And situations that may have appeared to be Either/Or decisions. One of the great values I observed was how much this helped to convert conflict into collaboration. It was magic! Contentious debates became reasoned conversations and teams began to think together in a newly constructed space of shared meaning.

A paradox of paradoxical reasoning is that you have been doing it your entire life and you likely don't realize that you have. I imagine that the lines from the Tao made complete sense to you even if it was the first time you read them. We constantly sort things and experiences into categories. IS and IS-Not is the most basic although it is often couched in the language of good and bad. It is mine and not yours. It is red and not blue. It is safe and not dangerous. These preferences and choices are both helpful and limiting. Our predefined patterns are efficient, and yet they don't always fit.

The simplicity of good/bad allows for a rapid response although sometimes a more nuanced view is helpful. This is especially true in social situations, with risky decisions, and where there is more than one right or useful answer or point of view, and when a conflict has become counterproductive.

I believe that paradox is a fundamental underlying building block of reality, meaning, and expression. The most basic building blocks of reality are things that exist and things that do not and for quantum theory folks, we know paradoxically that may be true and it may depend on an actor or observer. Paradox is a situational component of context comprising individual and social constructs. They are mental models of complex patterns of meaning and related choices that represent our realities. Through our belief in those representations, they are our realities.

There are many perspectives about the meaning of all this and we get to make up our own story as we like including asking and answering the bigger questions of universal experience, the meaning and purpose of life, time, consciousness, and creation. The purpose of this book is not to answer those questions although I'm convinced the tools of paradox can be applied, and that the theoretical and practical do finally merge into What Is. I am also sure that the tools of paradoxical reasoning and awareness can serve our immediate everyday needs within our lived experience of sensemaking and choices.

In the chapters that follow I will share a theory of Paradox with twelve underlying premises, half related to human sensemaking, and the other half to the role of paradox in that process. It is not the only theory of paradox or even the totality of everything that is related to this specific theory. It is a practical start on a path of thinking differently, of seeing more broadly and focusing more clearly. The theory is also the foundation for an approach to paradoxical reasoning and problem solving called Paradoxical Inquiry.

The focus of this work is three fundamental paradoxical questions and answers:

What is it and what does it mean?
The Paradox of Measurement and Understanding.

What do we want and who do we want to be?
The Paradox of Intention.

How do we benefit from what we know?
The Paradox of Awareness and Application.

Each chapter explores a foundational paradox that helps to answer these questions. You will see that paradoxes are used extensively to describe and explain the concepts and main points. This approach supports your practice of paradoxical thinking in a structured and natural way. At the end of each chapter there is a summary of main points and a Paradoxical Awareness Model that represents the chapter content. As this content is likely new for you, it may take a couple of chapters to start to make sense. That is typical when you are learning something new, be patient and reflect on the main points as you go. At the end of the book there is information for those interested in further study and professional use of the models.

As you practice this way of thinking it becomes very fluid. It is almost like a shorthand way of saying a lot in a small space. I particularly enjoy paradox as poetic expression; rain drops of wisdom on a parched plain of confusion if you like, or playful games as we go about the serious choices in life. These are building blocks to create and express ourselves. We can make anything we choose with them; we can create and multiply value, solve difficult problems, make conflict productive, and better understand situations, others, and ourselves.

Chapter 1

Close Enough, The Paradox of Measurement

Sacred wisdom and modern psychology remind us that we live and function in illusion. This isn't to say that we are unable to effectively navigate life, and in fact our approximate universe, or reality, is a feature of human perception not a bug. We are capable of extremely rapid response to environments with general perception and the capability to refine our measurement where it is needed. We do manage to get along in most instances although there are times when we can't see the forest for the trees or find ourselves taken in by a mirage. Where does this illusionary condition come from? It can be described as the paradox of measurement and meaning.

We can think of measurement as comprised of two general systems: perceptual measurement through our senses, and measurement tools. Measurement tools are technology-based mechanisms to extend our perceptual capabilities based on comparisons to some known standard. That can range from a rough estimate of inches based on the width of the human thumb to nanoscale observations based on laser applications in scientific instrumentation. Perceptual measurement is accomplished through our five senses and nervous system. These two systems of measurement enable us to have a sensemaking basis and ability to perceive, predict and modify our realities. In effect to collect the information that forms the basis of What Is.

While we have continuously improved our measurement technology over time from rough estimates to seemingly exact results, even the most sophisticated devices are accurate only within a tolerance range. Plus, or minus some small amount. Now in many cases that acceptable variance is very small, and practically unimportant, but nothing provides absolute accuracy. What these tools do provide are values that are close enough for our needs in the problem-solving situations we find ourselves in and where we intend to make some difference.

We have developed tools to help us see into realities we cannot directly perceive. Microscopes that can discern structures at the atomic level, imaging devices that can see inside our bodies, and telescopes that can see light from billions of miles away. In both the very large and very small contexts, the tolerances and limitations still hold true. As an example, our most recent advanced telescope can see further than ever before, and yet we can't see what those galaxies look like now. We are seeing them as they were when the light originated billions of years in the past and for now, that's as good as it gets.

The ability to measure is also significantly limited for direct human perception. We measure through our senses and nervous systems. These systems enable rapid responses to our environments, not exacting differentiation. The approximate answers our physical measurement systems, or senses, provide enable us to have an almost immediate (it feels immediate to us) approximation of our situations and what might be worth paying attention to in more detail within them.

An example is our visual data collection system. We operate in a range of light, the visual spectrum, but that is only a very small portion of what is going on in the environment. We perceive less than one percent of the electromagnetic spectrum, or all wavelengths of light, and that is generally good enough. Vision is a complex system that includes not only acuity over distance but also color perception and peripheral vison. Those aspects too are limited to ranges of color differentiation and fields of vision. Among individuals there is a further range of visual acuity from the very best possible human sight to complete blindness.

Our dogs hear and smell better than we do. Our tactile function has limited sensitivity. Microwaves are all around us, but we can't perceive them. Even with enhancement, our senses actually limit more information than they collect. That is a useful trait for an animal that must do something, make choices, and not be overwhelmed with the massive amount of information that is always going on around us.

Our selection and use of measurement tools depends on our awareness and access to options, our previous experience, and our ability to operate the tools accurately. We learn which ones to pick in each situation. These choices are habituated with repetition and success. Our choices always depend on what we want and what we can use. While there is truth in the common saying, when all you have is a hammer, everything looks like a nail, it is also the case that if you don't have a hammer, a rock, wrench, or pipe might just get the job done. We are both habitual and adaptable. We adapt to better, easier, and more preferred models and processes and then habituate them with practice and continued preference.

Our measurement tools also include models and frameworks, calculations, and theories. These contribute to the entirety of the physical and mental toolboxes that we have access to and employ. Reading this book is an act of perceptual data collection that enables use of the models and theories presented. Just as our realities are approximate, so are our theories and models. They allow us to make sense from large amounts of information and illuminate preferred actions.

Problem solving models and tools are extremely valuable and at the same time, when we approximate and summarize data, we have the potential to make it easier to understand and less of what is there. In fact, many models are based on a set of organizing sorting constructs, essentially, a built-in element of judgement of good or bad, right or wrong. A survey sorts people into predefined boxes and the characteristics applied to the box are then assumed about the person. Of course, the tools and theories are useful in sensemaking and just like physical measurement tools, they have tolerances.

Our senses are aware and alert without our focused effort. They can be consciously focused at will which is much easier than consciously turning them off. We are constantly taking in information and scanning our environments and occasionally we become consciously attentive. Oftentimes our first clue to a change or difference is a reaction that occurs before a conscious thought. We perceive a nearby threat, and before we process the facts, we have already recoiled.

Humans are the architects of our own realities. We are tool makers and users. We constantly build and adjust our patterns, or mental models, of reality. Sometimes this is purposive like reading a book or going to a class to learn something new or refine previous knowledge. It is also an automatic function and the foundation for our understanding. We seek new situations and patterns in work, play, and even when we are asleep. We are constantly learning and composing patterns, the lines in a message, steps in a recipe, notes and spaces in music, and the words and pauses in our speech.

Our individual perception depends on foundational characteristics just like the measurement tools. These dependencies describe the ranges of perceptual acuity, ability, focus and attention. The complexity of our entire world is summarized in our understanding with our own tolerances established by our human functions of mind and emotion, and the situations we experience and imagine.

We have two practical outcomes from measurement; as good as it gets, and close enough. On the surface these concepts may sound a bit fuzzy and subjective, and they are, while as rigorous as they can be or need to be. False precision can be as bad as limited accuracy especially when we are looking at solution options instead of one right answer. As good as it gets is based on the inherent limitations of technology and human perception. We are experiencing our environments with the senses we have. They are our only windows into this world and there are advantages and limitations with their acuity.

Close enough might be to the third decimal place, or repeated findings in multiple trials. The rigor is defined by the situation. It also considers the law of diminishing returns where continued rigor does not support a practical difference in understanding. As good as it gets is inherent in the measurement device, close enough is up to what I want and the opportunities and constraints within the situation and system.

We are extremely adaptable and a key to that adaptability is approximation. The major benefit to our flexible view of reality is that we can always enhance it and integrate new information, experience, and preferences into our existing models. We are essentially structured cognitively such that there is always room to grow, and we constantly are doing just that. This constant creation and modification of our mental patterns is the foundation and purpose of our human measurement system.

Chapter One Summary

- We perceive our environments through our senses and enhance those capabilities with tools that range from the very basic to the most sophisticated.

- The information collected approximates the complete environment, or reality, we experience.

- The variability among individuals in perception leads to a potentially infinite number of definitions of a situation.

Introducing The Paradoxical Inquiry Awareness Model: This model includes the Unity, Paradox Pair, Situational Dependencies, and Outcomes of a concept/construct. In the example, the concept is Measurement, the Paradox is Technology-Based Tools And Sense-Based Perception. These are supported by situational dependencies that shape the two outcome paradoxical synergy elements As Good as it Gets And Close Enough that contribute to the Unity Outcome of Results.

Unity

Measurement

Paradox

Sense-Based Perception And Technology-Based Tools

Dependencies

Availability And Usability

Accuracy And Cost

Conditions And Criteria

Attention And Automation

Accuity And Focus

Outcomes

As Good as it Gets, And Close Enough

Results

Chapter 2

It Depends, The Paradox of Understanding

The other side of the paradox of measurement and meaning is how we understand and create mental models of reality. Meaning of course is also a paradox. The paradox of assumptions and attribution, the mechanism for answering the question, "What is it and what does it mean?" The answer is always, "It Depends." It depends on the context/situation because that is where meaning is made, in our observed realities. It also depends on our personally accepted core reality. What we experience, and what we think and feel about it, is what it means.

A Human Being has approximately two and a half trillion cells, or about five times more cells than there are stars in the Milky Way. Both numbers are estimates because we don't have the means to know exactly how many in either case. These are currently as good as it gets approximations. No matter the exact number, the outer world's complexity is certainly mirrored in our own being and thankfully we only consciously manage a very small amount of that physical and mental self.

Like measurement, our meaning-based reality is also always an approximation and mostly created and managed automatically. Our autonomous nervous system takes care of the most important aspects of our human functions without conscious intervention including respiration, circulation, and digestion. We are so used to this that we hardly notice unless something goes wrong, or we stand back to observe ourselves. We are shaped by our natural selves, the patterns of growth and decay, emotional responses, drives and needs. We are also shaped by our experiences and acceptance of individual and social constructs, cultures and strongly held beliefs.

Our attention is automatic and purposive drawn. Try to notice the next time you have an itch and automatically scratch. The entire process from awareness to action is taken in an instant without a conscious thought or direction. The patterns of bodily functions exist in an interdependent system with massive complexity made from the most basic units of us, single human cells with our unique DNA patterns. The physical, cognitive, and emotional components that describe us, generally operate the same as our itch reflex, on their own.

We are animals and share traits with other animals, both close and distant evolutionary cousins. Life expands with amazing diversity and self-similarity. In effect, we are all forms, or expressions of animal life; humans, dogs, whales, and everything else. We start life not as blank slates but with instinctive knowledge and automated functions. We know how to be humans just like dogs know how to be dogs. It is written in our DNA, our own shared and unique patterns. An important framing aspect of meaning comes from our fundamental inherent patterns as social animals. Our needs for acceptance, status and contribution within our relationships and positions. We live and function in groups. We are part of patterns of dominance and subservience from family units and friendships to social activities like work and play.

We are constantly scanning our environments and when something catches our eye (warrants conscious attention) we seamlessly focus, although it may not be what we thought. These responses are very fast and for example, we might have a recognition of seeing someone we know at the market and only when we get a little closer do we realize we are wrong. For an instant the person fit the pattern of someone familiar until we gathered more information. Our understanding can be generally accurate while still open to many forms of misinterpretation. We make any number of mischaracterizations that we never question and for the most part we don't know it.

Even when we actively focus our attention and use cognitive processes to help make sense of things, our thoughts emanate from a layer below awareness, emerging as ideas in our streams of consciousness. Deep purposive thinking takes a lot of energy and is often supported by tools, heuristics, and habits of mind that we have learned work for us in those situations. The difference between purposive and automatic thinking is a paradox. Automatic thinking underlies and supports purposive thinking. It is the source of thought and the servant of our curiosity and needs. By the same token, purposive thinking is called upon as needed for gathering more information, sense-making when we are stuck or confused, navigating risky and novel situations, and making some choices.

In most cases we start the process of meaning making with an assumed predisposition model. Our preconditioned realities, or assumptions, include instinctual components, core desires like hunger and sexual gratification, biases, and emotional responses. We also have strongly held beliefs based on imprints from parents, family, and our early experiences, especially traumatic. These are reinforced and modified through further experience, practice, learning, and socialization including peer pressure to conform. These models create our frames of initial attention such that every new experience is grounded in our previous understanding and while we may be experiencing something unique, we maintain an overall perspective of illusionary stability, continuity, and control.

We are learning engines constantly taking in new information and adjusting our patterns without conscious thought. We might not conceive of it as a learning activity when we watch a video or listen to a song but consider for a moment the last program you watched. Can you describe the plot, what happened? I imagine you can, just like you probably know the words to many songs that just come to mind when you hear them. We don't normally say to ourselves, lets learn the story of this video or words to that song and we do learn it because that is how we work. That is also how we expand our knowledge and improve our thinking, through feeding our minds and seeding our memories with things we want to do and influences we desire to be more prominent. That can include self-improvement, spiritual practice, and reading this book.

The word bias may be characterized as something negative or bad. We are aware of many biases through the social constructs of racism, sexism, and others. In these cases, the biases represent a false view of reality that discriminates against others without true cause. Biases are inherently neither good nor bad. Like most patterns they are based on our experience and imprinting as shortcuts to meaning and rapid building blocks of situational awareness and action. They can be thought of as that myriad of preferences we have from the foods we like, our favorite activities, what to do in an emergency, and how to navigate with your boss. They are always summary approximations of something and therefore in any case fundamentally inaccurate and still useful. Forming these is an automatic component of our mental process and can be purposively altered through conscious effort, experience, and repetition when they impede our intentions.

We unquestionably accept our predispositions, biases and preferences, and do our best to inculcate them on others. We want them to see our points of view just as they would like us to see theirs. We are driven to achieve our own desires and prone to constant judgement about our progress and everything else. Even if we have no idea what something means, we will make an attribution that fits with our world view. In effect, if we don't know why, we will make it up. While assumptions characterize our initial framing of situations, attribution is our judgement of what they mean and why they occur.

The key to our approximate understanding of reality is this making it up process. While making it up might be characterized as creating false meaning as in telling a lie or twisting the facts, it is as good as it gets and close enough in most cases. We make up each experience, each day, and the story of our lives as we go. This may seem a little unsettling when we realize that not only us but our leaders, core influencers, trusted others, and loved ones are all also making it up as they go. We focus on some aspects of situations and miss or mischaracterize others. Without some purposive effort or a trigger to pay more attention, the lens of our initial frames of reference, biases, and desires provides a view of now and the future that is mostly a reflection of the past.

Remember, this is not good or bad, it is just how we work. This is an important realization. Good and bad are our judgements and sorting tools. They are the fundamental shorthand of judgement and in most cases the final level of attribution. Useful or not. Dangerous or not, I like it, or I don't. Very much Either/Or thinking. One of the fastest ways to arrive at meaning is to reject and we often do this without further consideration. If something doesn't fit our predefined picture or model, then it must be wrong. Wrong is bad and bad is reinforced as something to avoid.

It is important for us to be right, to be accepted, respected, and valued. We have jobs that pay us for doing the right thing, making the right objects, getting things done right on time, being influential with customers, and making the numbers. Choosing wisely is an advantage across our efforts and a life-long journey for many of us. This is incredibly important, and we don't leave it up to chance. Another paradox of attribution is that we do it internally and we make efforts also to manipulate, or influence, the perceptions, and attributions of others.

Like the initial mental frames of reference, we have for sensemaking we also have initial frames of social interaction and position. These are our personas or situational personalities. While much work has been done to describe human personality in a limited number of types or preferences it is likely unlimited in its potential for situational variation. We play roles based on what might be best for us. We conform to social constructs even if we dislike them or don't believe them to get along and get ahead. This is an advantage and a challenge. We are very capable of adopting the socially acceptable trappings expected of us in a situation. We are also mirrors to each other, adopting characteristics that we admire and strategies that lead to success with others, especially those with something we want or power over us.

Another thing we make up as we go is the story of why something happened and our role in the outcome. As most of this has been done automatically, we likely don't really know why we did most things. Sometimes we do know, and it would be socially unacceptable to share our motivations. Our personas act the necessary and appropriate part, presenting our attributions in a manner to reinforce with others that we made the correct choices and if not, why there was a good reason.

It is useful to remember a few of the many things that universally come naturally to humans. We may be encouraged by our parents but unless there is a disability, no one teaches us how to walk, or speak, or cry or sing. We just know how to naturally mirror our environments and accomplish what we are predisposed to do. Nor do we need to learn how to think. The underlying thought patterns that come to mind do that mostly with no purposive effort although we can direct them at will.

It is likely that we also engage in the process of sensemaking while we sleep. Our dreams and sleeping brain activity consolidate new information with previous patterns and fill in the blanks in our causal narratives. Dreams also preview choices, attempt to reconcile conflicts, and suggest action. Like dreams, meaning need not be based on observed factual agreements. Our realities need not be true to be real to us.

Our process of sensemaking leads to two outcomes: understanding and integration. Both are based on the situation, our past, and our desires. We integrate new experiences and knowledge, incorporating it into our frames of reference and from that process we create our personal understanding of what is. We have an automatic set of emotional reinforcement that goes along with this. We feel embarrassed or sorry when we make mistakes or fail, and we feel proud and energized when we win or appear to be right. We also have a full toolset of manipulating and influencing logic, personas, and emotions to support our goals as needed.

Our representations of the world made through observations are patterns and some aspects can be made with broad stereotypes and fine details added as needed. Much of meaning is a rapid matching of complex patterns that are approximate models. We naturally compare our current experiences to previous situations drawing similarities and differences. We practice this conscious process of meaning shaping as we construct new stories around things that have happened and those that we speculate could occur, things we want to happen, or just things that we imagine because we can, and these thought options are unlimited.

Chapter Two Summary

- Our realities are the result of a constant process of sense making that we make up as we go through life.

- Meaning making is mostly automatic and generally a constant process even when we sleep.

- Like all animals, we have instinctual patterns of meaning and social expectations related to our group roles.

- We make rapid situational assumptions based on our initial frames of reference that are constructed by patterns of biases, desires, and previous experience.

- We attribute causality, value, and utility based on our experience, core beliefs, desires, and social norms.

- Meaning does not depend on facts, it can be imagined, projected, and accepted from others.

Unity
Meaning Making

Paradox
Assumptions And Attributions

Dependencies
Nature And Nurture

Automatic And Purposive

Core And Situational

True And False

Observed Facts And Making it Up

Outcomes
Understanding And Integration

Meaning

Chapter 3

Two Sides of a Coin, The Paradox of Paradox

Our amazing brains are building models of reality constantly so that we can operate in the situations and environments we find ourselves in. This reality is full of dense connections and patterns formed from the contents of our memories and creations of our imaginations. The structure of meaning is based on patterns that are essentially fractal representations of Is/Is-Not observations. Those observations are instinctual and learned. Pattern construction is constant and revisionary. As we learn and experience new situations, we incorporate these into our existing patterns of contextual reality.

There is no limit to the creation of paradoxical relationships. Fundamentally, it can be anything that appears to be part of a situation. These are not inherently good or bad, right or wrong, accurate or inaccurate. They can be used to create greater understanding and to manipulate others. They are useful and can be destructive. They have no inherent moral core although they can be used to support a moral perspective.

An area where the power of associative creation is consistently used is in advertising where products are often shown in a context that creates a stronger meaning of value for possible buyers. Drug advertisements includes scenes of healthy people, and famous influencers lend their personas to products. Generally, the associations don't tell you more about the product, but they do create a bias to buy through connecting the product with a strongly held value, desire, or fear.

All patterns are related to context, even the ones we might claim are fundamental truths. For example, the paradox of good and evil is situated in the context of social behavioral expectations and the task of moral adherence in the conduct of one's life. It is a judgement framework that helps us navigate our situations, it is not the situation itself. That is why it is so important to understand the context because that is the situation and where we find the exceptions to the rule that might appear to us as paradoxical conditions or in effect something different than what we expected.

In current research from many disciplines paradoxes are typically described as opposite conditions. I would maintain that this is useful and a significant limitation. While in some cases they may be opposites, more likely than not they are two sides of a coin. In the case of paradox there are multiple typologies and perspectives that reflect theories of meaning and purpose. Each definition adds some clarity in another approximation of the phenomenon. A paradox of paradox is that these patterns of meaning are not tangible, even when they describe tangible or physical situations. In effect they don't exist outside of the mind of the observer and their only reality is what we ascribe to them just like any other pattern of meaning we hold in our individual and socially agreed realities. The impression that an association is unusual or unexpected is also based on the observer.

Earlier I described paradox based on attributes. I'll add a working definition for the purpose of communicating how I conceptualize this phenomenon. Like all previous models and theories, this is also an approximation although with a broader perspective to enable enhanced utility in understanding and problem solving. It is also a mirror of human sensemaking such that the theory is situated in how our minds work. We all have a theory of paradox even if we have never thought about it. My intention with the following definition is to establish a conceptual foundation for a system of structured work with paradox that can be shared, debated, enhanced, and improved.

A paradox is a contextually relevant meta-pattern, or schema, that includes an association of two large scale schemas that are elements of a unifying concept or unity. These large patterns include multiple other patterns and are also parts of even larger concepts that are situationally defined. These occur naturally and are created by making associations between events, conditions, and environments. The patterns are building blocks of reality from the most basic to the most complex. We make them up, they are provided to us by those who hope to influence us, and they exist as social constructs and distilled wisdom.

A theory is a supposition about the nature of something. It explains an aspect of our reality. In thinking about paradox an immediate and very important point is that we are not exploring the absolute nature of reality, we are looking at the nature of our individual and social realities as they exist within and among ourselves in specific contexts. Paradoxes describe reality but they are descriptions, abstractions, and constructs. They help us make sense of things even when they don't make sense. They enable us to see connections and dependencies with the result being an advantage of seeing more clearly and reacting more appropriately.

This theory is primarily philosophical. It is about the nature of human thought, meaning making, constructions of patterns of meaning, the limitations of these patterns, and the related action of choice making. I call it the Association and Unity Theory of Paradox. Below are a set of four hypotheses that describe the theory.

The Association and Unity Theory of Paradox

Paradox Hypothesis Statements:

One: Paradoxes are complex schemas representing an association of two situationally related concepts that form a unity of meaning.

Two: While paradoxes often represent seemingly discordant pairs, paradoxes function like any other complex association/ schema pair in situational meaning-making.

Three: Paradoxes are complex schemas or meta-patterns that are fractal in nature built upon and contributing to other levels of situational sensemaking patterns.

Four: Paradoxes like other complex schemas are individual and social, innate, and learned, and subconsciously and consciously created.

These hypotheses are supported by twelve foundational premises from research and practice. The first six describe aspects of human sensemaking and the second six describe the role of paradox in that process. As you read these, some may be contrary to your current perspective or counter to something you have learned. This paradox of paradox is related to how we think we think (metacognition) and how we use paradox to enhance critical thinking (paradoxical reasoning).

Foundational Human Sensemaking Premises:

1. Most human thought and behavior are automatic.

2. Meaning relies on context including contrived or imagined contexts.

3. All human meaning/sense making is an approximation.

4. Choices are made automatically and intentionally.

5. Human sensemaking is individual and social.

6. Meaning is described in patterns and mental models.

Foundational Paradox Premises:

1. Paradox is a phenomenon of human sensemaking.

2. Paradox is not limited to a single typology.

3. Paradoxes represent complex situational patterns.

4. Paradoxes are fractal-like mental models.

5. Paradoxes are individual and social constructs.

6. Paradoxes are informative, causal, and creative.

We will further explore paradox with the help of some simple structures. Remember that the structures and models are there to help us understand, not to limit that meaning. This paradox of explanation can be quite tricky and especially when we have preexisting assumptions that create automatic mental framing. Let's look at a simple example:

What is it? Of course, this is a line. What do we know about it? It has a certain size and length depending on how large the screen or book you are using causes it to appear, but there is no scale. It can also be noted that there is space above and below the line and they have no names. In most research and practice with paradox these lines represent opposite conditions. I would maintain that this is a point that obscures the view.

Instead of focusing on two polar opposites, we will imagine all of these lines to be made up of approximations of those characteristics from absolute fidelity to absolutely none of that characteristic, in effect between the beginning and end of the lines there is an infinite number of variations for any characteristic. While there may be an infinite number of variations, for paradoxes these are concepts not quantities. They are non-numeric and not continuous as the line might imply. One concept is not ½ of another, twice as much, or even in any specific order from more to less.

This two-dimensional view of paradox is useful for explanation and at the same time introduces a sense of relationships that may not exist. We see a linear explanation of complex non-linear concepts as if there is inherently a continuous relationship and order. We also tend to immediately ascribe values and judgements independent of the nature of the concepts represented. Above and below the line are similar to positive and negative and a numeric relationship is implied especially if we place a vertical line in the middle as is done in some representations of paradox. Like all representations and models, there is utility and limitations.

In my work with paradox these representations are useful for building awareness of the concepts, and I don't use them beyond that point. The awareness models also have a structure that is a conceptual flow describing a much more complex system of concepts and constructs. They are an approximation of the most prominent dependencies and outcomes with the potential to explore to a greater depth and broader view.

Often, we become aware of a paradox because we are stymied by some situation that appears to have conflicting or contradictory elements. In essence, an aspect of our sensemaking that doesn't appear to make sense. Paradoxes are mental patterns of some form or aspect of reality and artifacts of our sensemaking mechanisms. They are representations of our constructed reality. As such, they are as real and unreal as the rest of our mental models or schemas.

All paradoxes have a unifying characteristic or Unity and all Unities have underlying paradoxes. A framing point for our thinking about paradox is the awareness that most choices are not limited to a single either/or decision or even a more inclusive both/and perspective. Our choices more closely represent anything that we can imagine or want them to be. The framing we naturally use of limited choice is an illusion that is super-efficient and inherently limited in its accuracy. One of the beautiful things about conceived reality is it looks like it is all the ordered part of the same thing to us. As we are constantly modifying and adding new things into our stories of ourselves and our realities while it appears as if it is a stable experience when in fact the stability is that we are in a constantly changing environment that we regularly navigate just fine, with a great degree of general agreement, for the most part.

The concepts and constructs within paradoxes may also be combined in different associations with the same core attributes but different focus. Any specific association pairing reflects what is situationally relevant and any one concept or construct might be associated with anything else where appropriate. Some paradoxes appear in all instances of a situation or environment and others apply in several contexts and some in only a few. We can also build some generic models that can be finetuned in context remembering that we are always working with approximation and working toward close enough for the purpose at hand. The approximate models can be an efficient starting point for understanding and sharing.

We can think of paradox as opposites, mirror images, conundrums or things that shouldn't happen at the same time but do. We can also think of them as jokes, sacred distilled wisdom, or both at the same time. In all these modalities we end up with a statement/expression of a relationship that is connected and in many cases that connection is not obvious, and it might even appear to be troubling or even absurd. These unexpected associations or conditions may create or reflect a mental conflict. For our purposes we can define conflict simply as a difference that results in multiple choices. Conflict is neither good or bad, it just is and, in some cases, we live with it and in others we want to modify the outcomes that are related to the situation.

The possibilities are even greater. The potential for deeper understanding, collaboration, creativity, and synergy are also promises of paradoxical awareness and thinking. As paradoxes are not inherently positive or negative, they can be used to accelerate any intention through appreciation and support as well as manipulation and mistrust. In our contexts of application and consideration, it is up to us to decide what they mean and how we will use our understanding.

Chapter Three Summary

· The Association and Unity Theory of Paradox describes paradoxes as more than opposite characteristics. The broader perspective includes the unity that the two paradoxical elements mutually support as two sides of the same coin.

· Paradoxes are large scale schemas that are a natural aspect of sensemaking functioning as any other pair of concepts that contribute to a unity construct/concept.

· Paradoxes are neither good or bad, right or wrong, and the judgement as such is situational and based on the intention of the observer (individuals and social groups).

· Concepts and constructs have typical variations and may be combined with any number of other concepts to create an association pair or paradox.

Unity
               Paradoxical Commonality
Paradox
               One Thing And Two Things
Dependencies
               Intangible And Tangible
               Simple And Complex
               Finite And Infinite
               Individual And Social
               Conflict And Collaboration
               Synergy And Acceleration
Outcomes
               What it Is And What it Means
               Conceptual Reality

Chapter 4

Tolerances, The Paradox of Problems

Problem solving models and heuristics are supporting structures for systematic analysis of situations, issues, and future prediction. In most cases we look for a right answer to a problem we believe we understand with limited if any decision support framework. In most cases that works just fine. If the presenting question is, "What I should have for lunch?" and we are generally healthy and able to choose what we want it doesn't matter too much. Even if we don't really like it, we will eat again. But even this simple question like all things is embedded in a context. We need to understand more, like how much to spend and what foods to avoid because of allergies? One person's simple choice is another's complex problem.

Problems don't exist outside of context. The context, or situation, makes the problem when the outcomes and conditions are not what we prefer. There is not a world full of problems, there is a world full of situations that present choices. We create problems through our desires and preferences, effectively we want something different than the situation as configured currently provides.

One way to think about problems and appropriate problem-solving techniques is the concept of ill-structured and well-structured problems, another paradox. Generally, the difference is how much we know about the situation, if there are known and reliable methods to solve the issue, and if the issue has a specific solution. Of course, there are many other ways to look at problems through a paradox lens and these characteristics contribute to whether a problem is well structured or not. A few examples in paradox form:

Easy And Hard problems
Previously encountered And New problems
Problems we can solve And Problems that we can't
Newtonian problems And Quantum problems
Physical problems And Conceptual problems
One right answer And Many right answers

If you think about it, I'm sure you can add others. Well-structured and ill-structured problems also have typically different methods and solution types. Well-structured problems usually have a single most correct answer. What is the capital of Ohio? How many pints in three gallons? How far by interstate is New York from Los Angeles? What is the chemical composition of a known substance? Who took the last cookie in the box? What is the current reported sales for the month? How many children in a kindergarten class reported being hungry last week? Well-structured problems tend to have answers that are finite, specific, and stable or trending predictably over time. They are often numbers, categories, and names and are represented in measurable terms.

Ill-structured problems typically do not have an existing known answer, they are matters of opinion and debate. Often, they are missing key data and even a meaningful description. The answers are less stable and may represent uneven cycles and complex patterns. Where should we build the new plant? Who should we hire as the new CEO? How do I manage my remote team? How do we do something that has never been done before? How can we get along better? The answer to most ill-structured problems is – It Depends. It depends on contextual and preference factors, perspectives of observers and actors, history, social constructs, culture and the intentions of the problem owners and solvers. They may have layers of complexity and an answer that is a paradox and a continuing condition for balance and attention.

The two types of problems also work with approximation in different ways. A well-structured problem with an approximate answer will include boundaries for the answer in tolerances. For example, Part number A22 for product Alpha is 2.5 inches long plus or minus $1/32^{nd}$ of an inch. I would like 3 tomatoes give or take one for the luncheon salad. US size medium pants should fit men's waistlines from 32-36 inches. This is how products are designed and tested, quality control works, and general predictions are made based on historical data.

Ill-structured problems have a different kind of tolerance. It is the tolerance for other's ideas, perspectives, and preferences and the range of useful "right" answers. If there isn't a single right answer we can choose based on power, random assignment, or collaboration. These problems and answers are more dependent on social convention, culture, and status. I'm right because I'm the parent, the expert, the boss, or because I have been here the longest. We fix well-structured problems. Ill-structured problems may be chronic, random, and non-linear. They may also have answers that present many or even infinite solution sets. We don't fix these problems; we manage and balance them to support our preferences as much as we can. Essentially, solution options for problems are also a paradox; what it is (discreet absolute answer) and what we want (a range of options and choices).

It is important to match the problem-solving technique to the type of problem and situation and this starts with adopting an appropriate mental model or frame of reference. When we are practiced at problem-solving, we tend to do this from habit, or essentially an automatic response. This enables rapid solutions and sometimes it doesn't work. Those are the situations when we think it matches a previous pattern only to find out as we go that it does not. Paradoxically, this is a hazard of expertise and previous success. The assumption that we know what is wrong and how to fix it and that what we did before will work again.

Structured problem-solving ranges from hypothesis testing in research to mathematics, statistics, and even following a detailed recipe. Generally, it follows a process from awareness of an issue, problem definition including the context, identifying, and selecting solution options, solution implementation, resolution verification, and monitoring as needed. It is easy to create false precision goals and important to be aware of the law of diminishing returns. Remember rigor can be applied as needed and it can be optimized to stay within the practical and functional boundaries of close enough.

Does this mean that we should use more structure or process? Of course, the answer is, It Depends. The two primary conditions that create that dependency are what the situation is, and what we want. These can both be very simple and may also be very complex and this depends on the problem solver or solvers if done socially as in a work or family group. It also depends on the level of importance or risk, organizational and professional standards, and the purpose of the effort.

The concept of paradox is useful in understanding what kind of problem we are facing and what approaches will be helpful in arriving at a solution that matches our intention. It can also be helpful to use paradoxical methods for problem definition, analysis and discovery, presentation of findings, and ongoing contextual management and direction. The chapters that follow will focus on paradox and the application of paradoxical thinking to situations and problems where it can be practically applied to help create solution options that match our intentions.

A CEO once asked me, "How do you teach managers to make better judgements?" If I were to answer that question today, I would say, "Do it less often." Judgement is a valuation of actions, people, and choices. Its typical outcome is a determination of good and bad, success and failure, worth and waste. It is very helpful and like all things less so when overused. A basic Paradoxical Awareness Model of this process is below.

Unity
>
> Judgement

Paradox
>
> Right And Wrong

Dependencies
>
> Measurement And Observation
> Assumptions and Attributions
> Correct And Incorrect
> Expectations And Outcomes
> What you Want And Not What you Want

Outcomes
>
> Good And Bad
> Value

This model is appropriate for well-structured problems when we are comparing a current state to a definitive standard. The judgements are a sorting process between conformity and non-conformity. The approach is not wrong, and the utility depends on the type of judgment/choice we are trying to make. This takes us back to the kind of tolerances we are working with and whether we are using linear problem-solving or not.

You can see why it would be easy to become frustrated when you have a process that works, and you are not aware that it isn't always the appropriate approach. This is a common problem for individuals who go from being experienced technical problem solvers to roles where they must judge ill-structured problems including multiple options, unknown situations, and the complexities of people management.

In judging outcomes in ill-structured situations, the Paradoxical Inquiry model is a better fit. We start with What Is and make an effort to defer judgement until we consider the characteristics and dependencies with a neutral evaluation.

Unity
                        Evaluation
Paradox
                  What Is And Intention
Dependencies
               Performance And Aspiration
        What's going Well And What would you Change
                  Current State And Future State
                  Close Enough And Good as it Gets
Outcomes
                     Nudge And Monitor
                          Action

From a disciplined inquiry perspective, we are moving from a research paradigm to an evaluation paradigm with a twist. The difference being that typically in evaluation practice we describe outcomes as formative or summative, in-process or final. Given the continuous flow of changes in complex systems and understanding, we recognize that in effect there are not final judgements at all, only iterations of approximation, intention, and adjustment guided by the tolerances of close enough and as good as it gets.

In both models we arrive at a place where we make choices. We choose to act and to defer, between alternative actions, to do it ourselves and to involve others. A few guiding conditions for action include the below in paradox form.

What you Control And What you don't Control
What is Urgent And What can be Deferred
What is Transitory And What is Long-Term
What you Know And What is Unknown
Doing Something And Doing Nothing
Doing it Yourself And Letting Others Do It
Taking a First Step And Taking a Next Step

This set of conditions supports the initial statement of Do it Less Often although the choices paradoxically still require judging what to do and what not to do. In that past conversation my advice at the time to the CEO was to let them practice with monitoring feedback. Now, I would also add this background understanding represented in the awareness model below to support performance guidance and feedback based on the person and situation.

Unity
                    Performance Management
Paradox
                        Novice And Expert
Dependencies
                    Known And Unknown
                    Important And Trivial
                    Simple And Complex
                    Trust And Doubt
Outcomes
                Active Support And Passive Control
                    Managerial Attention

This model considers the experience of the person, the degree of problem definition, and the importance of that choice. It also looks at the level of trust the leader has in the subordinate. Trust and Doubt are a filter. If there is doubt, then increase support, and with trust relax control. A useful precept I believe is that doubt indicates that you need to help, not that you judge the person as failing, and trust means to loosen control so they can advance their practice.

We start the process of problem solving with a set of usually unconsidered assumptions that often include a ready-made solution set. We think we recognize the problem, and we head down the path of familiar solution. This initial consideration frame is the beginning of a process of fault isolation and remediation. People tend to have preferred problem solving approaches and apply them to most of their issues.

We are habituated to believe that problems have correct answers. Think of all the years in school where you practiced finding the one right answer. In my teaching I often present problems with many solution options. This is a more realistic outcome and sometimes quite frustrating for students as they are so used to the treasure hunt for the one best right answer.

Problem solving efforts typically are bound by an assumption of opportunities and constraints that influence everything from the decision to do something, what methods to use, and the general solution. In some cases, an issue is presented, and an immediate effort ensues to identify best practices or benchmark results. In other cases, in organizations with the practice, it becomes a Lean and Six Sigma investigation. Maybe a certain person is identified because of their previous success in similar problems. It is very common to immediately start throwing out solutions on cursory observation of issues and those might be immediately adopted because what is currently going on looks like something we have seen before. We also eliminate options as things we tried before but didn't work.

Unity
>Consideration Boundaries

Paradox
>Opportunities And Constraints

Dependencies
>Known And Unknown
>Situation And Information
>Urgency And Importance
>Individual And Social
>Power And Influence

Outcomes
>Considerations And Limitations
>Problem Space

The pool of opportunities and constraints in any situation is potentially infinite. Like most paradoxes individuals tend to have a preference for one or the other. In this case one example is the common observation that people are "glass half full," or "glass half empty," or characterized as optimists and pessimists. Thinking of this as a paradox the nature of the concept is that in all situations there are opportunities and constraints. There are more in both cases than we consider, and it is also likely that any contributing factor is actually both an opportunity and a constraint depending on the situation.

The dependencies that are prominent have the greatest influence on the outcomes of what is considered and what the general boundaries for the problem definition and solution sets will become. This degree of influence is based on who is involved from a single person's mental models to a larger social group and the collective wisdom. Generally, three conditions describe these dependencies: the situation, assumptions, and choices. Essentially, from onset to completion, problem definitions and solution possibilities are framed by what we think it is and what we want.

Chapter Four Summary

- Most of our problem solving is done informally without the assistance of formalized structure or methods.

- We habituate successful problem-solving approaches and replicate them when we think there is a match between a situation and previously encountered issue and solution.

- Well-structured problems have known conditions and typically have a single correct answer. Ill-structured problems may have many possible solutions and have a range of approximate solution options.

- You fix linear well-structured problems, and the situation is no longer a problem. You balance conditions and paradoxes to acceptable levels of performance.

- Solutions are framed by what it is and what we want.

Unity

Problem Solving

Paradox

Ill Structured And Well Structured Problems

Dependencies

Linear And Complex
Standards And Approximations
Comparison And Discovery
Mechanistic And Quantum
One Answer And Many Options

Outcomes

Fix And Balance
Solution

Chapter 5

Sand in Our Oyster, The Paradox of Conflict

Conflict occurs naturally when there is a difference of perspective and intention in a situation. This can be internal to ourselves, in a family, social unit, or any other level of human organization. As stated previously, it not inherently good or bad although it is typically characterized as such. Oftentimes we try to avoid conflicts and are afraid. Sometimes we create them and use that fear as a means of controlling others. Conflict can lead to actions that range from mild disappointment that I'm not getting my way to large scale violence.

Conflict can also be driven by love, appreciation, and concern for others. It can be the motive force for new understanding, novel approaches to problems, and creative expression. Our greatest achievements are rooted in the conflict between what was and what was possible. It can be the awareness that leads to breakthroughs and previously unimagined achievement. It is natural part of growth and change and an energy to fuel our creativity.

You and I may even be involved in a conflict right now as you read this if you have a difference in opinion with what I'm stating. Conflict is just difference, the difference between what we know and what we learn, the past and the present, and every choice that has more than one option. It is a critical element of the plot to our stories and the stories of our lives. Every conflict really does inherently contain both the seeds of destruction and creativity.

Let's consider some positive expressions of conflict that we enjoy. These are ubiquitous and a few examples include sporting events, trivia contests, playing cards, the myriad of professional food challenges, livestock championships, and spelling bees. In our professional lives we have differentiated awards for employees, salesperson of the quarter, and are motivated by performance races with peer companies for the best rates of margin and growth. Personally, we have the completion of the degree program, a competitive promotion, and maybe even making sense of what all this paradox stuff means.

Individually these are a constant part of our lived experience from the unresolved past to the unknown future. We set goals for ourselves, compete to be our best, and work to understand something that is unfamiliar as we learn. We also judge these experiences as good or bad based on the alignment of the outcomes to our intentions. This, like our other mental processes, occurs both automatically and purposively, mostly unconsciously and occasionally with full awareness.

Conflict is a creative condition that underlies our choices and guides our actions. It is the sand in our oysters that creates our pearls and the grit in the gears that impedes our progress. It is fun and painful. It is also constant and therefore an energy to use, learn from, and apply in support of where we want to go and what we want to achieve. Another interesting aspect of conflict; it draws energy with continuation. The minor spat that ends with someone sleeping on the couch. The festering issue that divides families and work groups, and the border incident that provokes war. The energy isn't just that of negative escalation. It can also result in positive power. The power of achievement, satisfaction, and competitive advantage. Think of the heroic turnarounds of a business, the completion of a shared struggle, the coaches pep talk at half-time that results in the winning goal, and the months of diet and exercise that finally result in a desired weight loss.

When we apply a basic paradoxical inquiry approach, we start with What Is, the intention, (what do you want and who do you want to be), and work to realize Our Solution instead of My Way or Your Way. A benefit of this practice is that some of the major underlying conflicts are revealed, and a common understanding is achieved. While the conflict likely does not go away, learning to see it differently is a fundamental benefit from this practice and awareness. Understanding the connections and dependencies creates leverage and synergy.

I must also recognize how the opposite effect is achieved as it is very common. This is the use of defined opposites (true or not) forming the basis of vilification and adoration. This is widely done and easily recognized especially in political discourse. Political refers to any social power structure, not just governments. It runs on hate and fear and works. It is the path of the demigod, autocrat, and dictator.

It is not my intention to empower hate, destruction, and separation. I doubt they need my assistance. I am very interested in supporting the balance of perspectives, mutual benefit, and the creation of massively more value. I also know that both sides of an argument can be augmented with good intention and lift both perspectives from destructive to constructive. This is an important reminder, we do tend to have a preferred side of the debate and the challenge is much less supporting our perspective, it is seeing the value and possible benefits of the side we oppose.

This starts with the simple recognition that it is possible. It is possible to find inner peace and outward cooperation. We can understand the truth within even the most egregious lie, and we can find our way together. We can support competition and cooperation at the same time and benefit from both consistent with our intentions. This is the synergy of our unities. In order to improve outcomes from social conflicts, we really only need to answer a few simple questions:

- Where am I? (My condition/context)

- What do I want? (My intention)

- What are the seemingly opposed contextual and social conditions?

- Where is the possible agreement and synergy?

- What is the outcome we collectively desire?

- What would we nudge to move toward this new state?

We can use the Awareness Model to describe the conflict which is the two paradox components and name the unity that unites the two perspectives. Just realizing the connection can be a major path to improvement. The conditions are the dependencies, and finally the outcomes possibilities for the paradox pair. With a statement of intention and a quick review of what is working (what we want) and what could be changed and improved we have options for nudges. These are always an approximation and the social agreement on the terms and conditions itself is very useful in reframing the conflict from good/bad to What Is and What We Want. The goal is a closer approximation to Close Enough and the collective understanding of the situation and possibilities.

Let's look at a simple example in business. The paradox of Centralize and Decentralize. This is a regular conflict between the home office and remote sites, or the boss and her reports. This paradox describes the concept of distributed authority. Centralization and decentralization as a concept just are; they exist in all organizations and relationships. There are times when it is best to centralize and times when it is best to decentralize. Both are right (good or bad) in their time and there are infinite gradients between the poles of the two.

This is a very important realization – the paradox is not a problem; it is a universal condition. The problem is when our intention requires a different set of choices in how we express/ manage our response; when our pattern of response no longer fits what we want. We start this with something that doesn't seem right, and instead of writing it off, or living with an uncomfortable conflict, we can work together for a better result.

Keeping the example of centralize and decentralize, we want to provide same day service but our scheduling office in Denver takes two days to process the order and arrange the call. Now we might be inclined to propose that we decentralize this activity and do it at every location to cut time, a logical response. You may have experienced this type of unconscious paradox management where we just pendulum between one and the other and just when it seems like we have it right we change again. This happens often too when a new person joins the team and brings well-intentioned solutions from previous experience that don't particularly fit here.

Even if we have done this before we must see if the situation has changed. Our conflict often arises because we have two or more opinions vying to be "right" and the challenge is that they are all right depending on the situation. If we allow ourselves to listen to ideas through this lens, we lay the groundwork to think together about what we both want that will work even better for all of us.

Our goal here is to share meaning to arrive at shared meaning. We must share our perspectives and observations as the basis for any agreement and explore the context to better understand the situational characteristics that will direct our choices. Discussing this as a paradox that we balance reduces the personal tension. There is an admission that all points are valid, and our effort is only to choose. This isn't what we usually want to do. We just want to find a quick pattern that matches and call it a day. If it is important enough, then we need to slow down and do the work of thinking about the situation enough to improve our choices and related outcomes. Maybe enough even to give us a competitive advantage.

Let's go back to our example, if we think together, we might find that there are some essential components of the transaction that really do need to be done in Denver in some specific cases – it meets a criterion of escalation for approval, and for those cases a two-day turnaround is close enough. Similarly, in a significant number of cases it is fine to make a local choice with the one-day turnaround expectation. This is what we are looking for, how do we get the best of both centralize and decentralize possibilities to support our goals and intention. As we understand the situation and explore our ideas together, we lay the groundwork for connecting on common agreement.

We then set the stage for agreed outcomes using the two parts of intention. In our example this could be Competitive Service And Efficient Operations or Rapid Service And Smooth Operations. The goal is to describe what we want together. These are not aspirational statements or new metrics. They are statements of practical possibility that get us in a range of choices that is close enough and an awareness that as the situation changes, we will adjust. Conflict is a great trigger for reflection. It is a signpost to destruction and opportunity and new choices. With awareness we can see the possibilities that help us to realize our intentions.

The example reveals another common source of conflict related to change over time and overuse. I refer to this condition as, "You Should Until You Shouldn't." There are two primary versions of this. The first is when over time conditions change and a perfectly acceptable outcome no longer occurs because the dependencies have changed, or the intention has evolved. The second case is the classic too much of a good thing when something positive becomes an extreme version or too great of an influence in relation to other aspects of the system. We see this all the time. I love ice cream and I probably should not have it after every meal. It is sometimes easier to do something yourself other than help another person learn, or we just get our way too often and inadvertently inhibit the growth and value of others. These are the situations where something that seems bad or wrong has a seed of truth, previous value or possibility that has grown beyond its usefulness.

Practice observing conflict and listening to your own triggers like getting annoyed or mad. Where is the opportunity? How do you apply your will to affect a positive result. This is not an excuse for overlooking dangerous attacks. It is a moment of reflection to remind us to not be defensive or aggressive in those normal everyday disagreements that can result in damage to relationships, reputations, and future collaboration. This may take some practice and be ready to forgive yourself and others when the emotion gets the best of you and them.

In business we want to delight customers, fully engage employees, and maximize shareholder value. It feels like we must pick one and give up the others. This is the classic Win/Lose equation. Another choice is for us to compromise until we get to a choice we can live with. No one gets what they want. Let's recognize that Win/Lose and Lose/Lose are not our only options. In fact, we can even go beyond Win/Win to Win/Win/Win/Win as we align the benefits from our efforts across as many contributors as possible in the magnification of value.

Chapter Five Summary

- Conflict occurs naturally when there is a difference of perspective and intention for a situation.

- Conflict can be the motive force for new understanding, novel approaches to problems, and creative expression.

- Conflict draws energy with continuation.

- Paradoxical approaches to conflict are not inherently positive or negative.

- The simple recognition of the possibilities of conflict provides an initial level of value.

- A simple paradox approach is useful as well as the more structured processes of Paradoxical Inquiry.

- Conflict can be a trigger to identify opportunity.

- The outcome from conflict can be massive value throughout the chain of contributors and benefactors.

Unity

Conflict

Paradox

Difference And Perspective

Dependencies

Advantage And Barrier
Constructive And Destructive
Individual And Social
Engagement And Avoidance

Outcomes

Opportunity And Leverage
Energy

Chapter 6

Double Vision, The Paradox of Awareness

How do we benefit from what we know? The answer is the Paradox of Awareness and Application. Awareness can be described by the paradox of perception and intention. We recognize paradoxes with an intention of benefit consistent with what we want.

Unity
> Awareness

Paradox
> Perception And Intention

Dependencies
> Bias And Discovery
> Insight And Meaning
> Personal And Social

Outcomes
> Recognition And Understanding
> Clarity

With our awareness, we can pull things together, see the big picture and provide more value. We can also see pinch points, dependencies, and leverage opportunities. We can understand other's points of view and instead of opposing them find agreement. We can also build a common reality. It is the foundation of synergy and creative effort and the realization of individual and group possibilities.

I believe there is massive value in just being able to recognize that these exist. There is advantage in being able to see the two sides of an argument, relationships between concepts in a system, and the gaps in a single view. Noticing Both/And instead of Either/Or is as easy as listening for how associations are characterized. Another simple tool is to ask yourself if there is another side to your point of view or position. Hear the connections you make with concepts as you try to support your position and convince others to agree. If you begin to consider the possibility that there are indeed at least two sides to everything, you will start to see them.

As a summary to each of the chapters in this book, I have employed a simple model of paradoxical awareness. With a little practice these become easy to construct. These approximate statements of situational reality start with either a paradox statement; the two parts, or the unity they support; the two sides of the coin and the coin. The models I have shared are based on my understanding and you may see them somewhat differently. That is OK, since meaning is situationally created and relevant, my approximation may be a little different than your view. At the same time the simple models create that opportunity to see a deeper layer of meaning. The power in the model is that it provides a framework for personal and social understanding, agreement and action.

The paradox component of the model is a prominent contributor to the nature of the unity. Concepts have many situationally relevant components, and some are more prominent than others. Think of the models as flowing from what a concept is (The unity) to what the outcomes are that result from choices related to it (Outcomes). In between the two there are dependencies that shape the nature of the outcome. What the nature of the outcomes are, depends on these prominent dependencies.

Paradox can be integrated into many efforts from choosing priorities to evaluation of performance. Remember, if there are linear problems, use those tools. If there is a single right, or as good as it gets answer, rely on those. If there is not, then there are paradox possibilities. I use the Paradoxical Awareness Model as a teaching tool in university courses. The simple model describes a complex system in a very accessible way. Another variation of that model I've used describes the Purpose, Processes, and Outcomes of a business or function. The example below is from a testing and certification organization.

The Company (name withheld)

Purpose

Certification And Knowledge

Process

Standards And Accreditation

Testing And Validation

Audits And Training

Required And Voluntary

Trust And Honesty

Outcomes

Third Party Evaluator And Business Partner

The next example is one I used in a graduate research course comparing the paradigms of research and evaluation. These are very similar in process, and dissimilar in outcomes which can be confusing for students. The simple model makes it easy to see what the common components are and the differences that separate the two approaches that share methods.

Unity
>
> Scientific Inquiry

Paradox
>
> Research And Evaluation

Dependencies
>
> Qualitative And Quantitative
> Validity And Reliability
> Assumptions And Attributions
> Observations And Measurement
> Data And Analysis
> Scholarship And Practice

Outcomes
>
> Discovery And Judgement
> Results

These models represent a complex system in a succinct fashion. They are inherently judgement free although there is normally a preference for one side of the other of the paradox statements. These are useful for building self-awareness, sharing concepts, and fundamentally reinforcing the Both/And connections. The next model is based on a book I wrote entitled Leadership From Below, Paradoxes of Submarine Leadership. I used the model as an analysis framework to reveal management paradoxes that contribute to the high performing environment of submarine operations.

Unity
>Submarine Leadership

Paradox
>Trust And Doubt

Dependencies
>Courage And Fear
>Daring And Caution
>Individual Responsibility And Teamwork
>Frivolity And Seriousness
>Criticism And Support
>Hierarchy And Social Norms
>Teachers And Learners
>Change And Stability

Outcomes
>Leadership And Management
>Mission Accomplishment

This model describes shared dependencies for every member of the crew although the exact nature of that effort depends on the role and rank/level of the crewmember. These are also possibilities for high performance in any organization and the leverage potential revealed in the model is a good start for thinking about possibilities.

Paradoxes can be based on conflicts, conditions, and also possibilities. The models describe the flow of choices/concepts that create the quality and performance of the outcomes. The same model exists for the most part in high preforming and low performing organizations, the difference is the influence of the dependencies and situational prominence of aspects of the dependencies, the contributions each side makes toward the desired state.

The next model is based on a recognized conflict between operational budgeting and longer-term investment.

Unity

Financial Planning

Paradox

Short-Term Budgets And Long-Term Strategy

Dependencies

Alignment And Integration
Timeframe And Specificity
Communication And Authority
Execution And Vision
Intention And Interpretation

Outcomes

Investment Choices And Team Alignment
Direction

This model describes the concept of Ethics.

Unity

Ethics

Paradox

Moral and Legal

Dependencies

Behavior And Patterns
Standards And Culture
Judgment And Flexibility
Situation And Mitigating Factors
Accidental And Purposive

Outcomes

Right And Wrong
Guidance

Let's play with making an example with a common concept that is often presented as a source of conflict. Remember these are often described as if they are opposed in an Either/ Or choice when more likely they are connected summaries of many concepts and choices. They are not inherently right or wrong, good or bad. In this example the Unity (or coin) is Government Purpose something that can be a major source of conflict and disagreement.

The next level of description should be as inclusive as possible to describe the Unity construct, a paradox that captures an essential large-scale pattern the defines meaning in the context of use. My selection for the core paradox is Individual Rights And Collective Good. This is a large-scale prominent aspect of the unity, and this paradox is a dependent pair that represents the basis for related choices. It is inherently judgement neutral, both sides are sources of value although there are situational and personal preference biases between the two.

The awareness model now looks like this:

Unity
                    Government Purpose
Paradox
          Individual Rights And Collective Good

The next step is to describe some of the dependencies or building block concepts that apply in shaping the paradox to represent choices based on the intention of the user(s). This is an analysis process and as you practice, it becomes rapid and second nature. There can be many or just a few and just like earlier, these will describe large patterns that influence the reality of the paradox statement.

Dependencies

Safety And Security

Opportunity And Options

Respect And Affiliation

Fair And Equal

Earned And Inherent

Stable And Responsive

Citizen And Country

These characteristics are drivers of perspectives within the paradox. If we were interested in doing multiple layers of analysis, we could continue by layer with each paradox pair having its own Unity. This works in the same fashion for building bigger concepts and drilling down for more detail. For example, Earned And Inherent could describe the Unity of Benefits. The final part of this diagram is one more paradox. The paradox of outcomes describes the core choices that result from the perspectives based on individual intention.

Unity

Government Purpose

Paradox

Individual Rights And Collective Good

Dependencies

Safety And Security

Opportunity And Options

Respect And Affiliation

Fair And Equal

Earned And Inherent

Stable And Responsive

Citizen And Country

Outcomes

Personal Value And Social Value

Benefits

In this example, we can see in the dependencies the perspectives, assumptions, and choices that influence the nature of the outcomes. You might also be able to see areas of possible agreement and further understanding. Both sides of the dependencies also represent broadly recognized value that would not be as obvious if focused only on one side or the other. This is a very complex issue and every one of the dependencies presents an opportunity for a Both/And perspective and potential increased general value that doesn't require taking something from one side to add to the other.

The utility of the awareness model is its ability to help us understand situations, influences and choices. It does not present concepts as good or bad or right or wrong. There is no inherent judgement. There is always value in both aspects, and the opportunity to use this awareness to move toward a more generally preferred state.

Some of the examples in this chapter refer to a specific situation (the investment conflict), some refer to a class of situations (Submarine leadership), and some to a generic concept (Ethics). The last example represented a new way to look at a long entrenched social conflict. The models have a practical purpose which is to describe and reveal the conflicts and serve as a means to create common understanding. They are always approximations and since that is the case, any debate is only about what is present and prominent and how can we benefit to the greatest extent possible.

The models can be a great starting place for gathering feedback and clarification from other perspectives. I think they are also really effective practice tools to develop paradoxical awareness. It is easy to find practice opportunities, just look for any type of conflict. You can start building these with your own perspectives and personally relevant conflicts.

Chapter Six Summary

- Paradoxical awareness can be described by the paradox of perception and intention. We recognize paradoxes with an intention of benefit consistent with what we want.

- Our awareness is the foundation for understanding what is, and where we intend to be able to influence that toward a preferred condition.

- Our thinking is not constrained by an absolute good or bad and therefore it is important in all of these things to see through/with our intention.

- Awareness is an automatic and purposive process and with simple effort you can create a closer approximation.

- The Paradoxical Inquiry Awareness Model can be used to reveal, understand, and predict conceived realties.

Unity

Awareness

Paradox

Perception And Intention

Dependencies

Bias And Discovery
Insight And Meaning
Personal And Social

Outcomes

Recognition And Understanding
Clarity

Chapter 7

Alone and Together, The Paradox of Shared Meaning

Paradox is the language of agreement. It creates the opportunity to have a closer common understanding of shared reality. There is exponential power in shared thinking and massive efficiency in agreement, alignment, and commitment.

Unity
Shared Meaning

Paradox
Together And Alone

Dependencies
Alignment And Commitment
Appreciation And Affiliation
Fear And Trust
Teaching And Learning

Outcomes
Social Agreement And Aligned Intentions
Common Understanding

Consider the paradox of together and alone. I believe that it is unfortunately too common that we separate ourselves and others, and like the separation of concepts, there are unrecognized synergistic unities within social groups and relationships. In effect, I believe that we are always together and alone at the same time. We are unique individual human beings who are social animals with aspects of shared realities based on our cultures and contexts. We mirror each other and adopt social norms and mores. We have formal and informal social hierarchies and roles, and we derive great value from our social affiliation and contributions.

Sometimes I'm told by senior leaders that they can't work along with their teams because others will be intimidated and not think freely. This is quite a self-criticism. My advice is just try, and know that no matter what, authority is not reduced by thinking together. The opposite comes with that, accelerated performance from social agreement and enhanced perspectives from multiple views. The views of others who are closer to the processes and outcomes form a whole that is familiar to us all and a closer total approximation of the context/situation.

There is no need to withhold social value out of fear that another person might get used to it or abuse the privilege. Why not try in every situation and condition to achieve our intention and be bounded only by as good as it gets and close enough. Laying the groundwork for thinking together requires an effective balancing of the fear and trust paradox. I'm not saying it requires the elimination of fear. Fear like everything else, isn't inherently good or bad. Sometimes it is situationally less preferred when our intention prescribes and sometimes it fits. This is especially true if you think of fear as a combination of excitement and concern which underpins both being afraid and being daring.

When we are in social situations and perceive a threat, it is natural to become defensive and maybe even return the anger, dirty look, or minor insult. It takes practice but being able to feel the trigger and maintain an open defenseless position is a major advantage. The important aspect to perceive is what is this telling me? In this situation, what does it mean? Emotions are useful ques for both satisfaction and conflict. We don't need to attempt to tightly control normal emotional responses, instead we can leverage them for greater understanding, empathy, and ultimately success.

Paradoxically, a sense of urgency sometimes is a great barrier to rapid success especially when we jump to conclusions and solutions. A special challenge is created through an unwillingness to think together. An example is when leaders say, "Don't bring me problems, bring me solutions," to reports who lack experience and problem-solving skills. The other side of this paradox is abstaining from having an opinion or contributing because you are not the boss. Remember that our shared goal is as good as it gets and close enough based on our intentions and we all share that responsibility. We also want to minimize confusion, wasted time, unproductive conflict, and damaged relationships.

There is some very good news related to thinking together. We already know how to do it. I remember when I was a little boy playing pretend games with my brother who was a year and a half older than me. With no training, structure, or knowledge of what we were doing, we created the backdrops for our imaginings, and we did it together. We seemed to know what each other was thinking in the flow of play. I imagine you still play just like I do. It might be a little different in form but, in its essence, it is the same. I like to think of the unity of play as containing the paradox of Fun And Creation. We enjoy ourselves and make things.

We make patterns of conceptual reality even when expressed as physical forms like products and structures. We love patterns, we think in patterns, and we are amused and entertained by patterns. Fundamentally, we are patterns both physically (DNA) and mentally (mental models and schemas). All things we play are patterns. Think of a few simple examples, playing cards, chess, and boardgames. Listening and playing the patterns of music. Competing within the structure of basketball or soccer in patterns of performance and rules.

We go to the theater to see plays that are based on a pattern called a script or story. The pattern of stories is central to our memories and our awareness of our experience. We tell the stories of our lives, our dreams and our beliefs. The narratives of history are constructed for businesses, families, and countries. Problems are also stories, what happened, what was the impact, who did it, and who fixed it.

I'm telling you a story right now as you read this even though I'm not physically present and we may never meet. In a sense we are remote playmates as I present concepts and you create personal meaning. We are both making up something that didn't exist before. It is likely occasionally challenging, and I hope a bit of fun for both of us as we play teacher and learner. The two of us also play both roles. I'm learning as I share with you, and you are teaching yourself. We are all teachers and learners in the end as we construct meaning from new situations and experiences based on a foundation of what we already know and believe.

Don't be fooled by the term play as something trivial. World class athletes, chess masters, investors, artists, educators, and businesses all play a game. Some based on strict rules and protocols and others in free form as they explore new horizons and possibilities. Actually, it is all play, and we are all making it up as we go just like my brother and I did when we were little boys. It also has the same possibility for wonder and joy.

As stated previously. when you first realize this, it can be a bit unsettling. Authority figures, parents, and all manner of experts are making things up. Some with very strict structures and others pretty much winging it. They may have a purposively developed set of concepts and experiences to enable performance including in some instances achieving certain credentials to practice in the games they choose. Some games are very difficult and sometimes it is hard to understand the rules. Some require innate talents and physical skill. Some games we can play by ourselves and most games we play socially, like the games of school and work.

Of course, another thing happens when we think. and play together, we reinforce that we value each other. It is very affirming to be listened to and have your ideas considered. It is a great reward that has no cost and massive value. With practice we learn how to let down some of our protective barriers and reduce the limitations of power difference and preconception. We can share what we think and do it in a way that others can understand. Using the neutral framework of paradox inherently reduces the noise, fear, and mistrust that occurs especially in risky and important choices. It moves groups away from who can talk loudest or defaulting to what the boss thinks to shared contribution and common understanding.

In paradox workshops an amazing transformation occurs on the very first day often before lunch. Individuals who came in as co-workers are now colleagues even those who have just met. I attribute this to an opportunity to think together. Not just work together or have discussions, really think together as they consider a paradox relevant to their shared success. The task is different, the approach is different, and the management of the time is different. All these things are like this to encourage social cognition. The active creation of a revised shared reality that is collectively a closer approximation to their situation than any one person's initial mental model.

Looking together through a paradox lens allows us to move beyond trying to fix things that are not linear problems and provides an approach that is natural, and simple, for systems thinking. The framing of complex associations with paradox is also fun. It is cognitively stimulating, and everyone can play. Our goal is to achieve a commitment to social agreement on an approximate answer that is aligned with our intentions.

Within the unity of commitment is the paradox of dependability and dependence. I imagine dependability seems right if this is the first time you have heard this and dependence maybe not so much. These two concepts describe the agreement of commitment. I perform and behave in a dependable manner and my reward is being able to depend on the benefits of that performance. Benefits might mean salary and respect, belonging and attachment (affiliation), and even affection and acknowledgement (appreciation).

Our realities are continuous and while we might have situational personas and intentions, we are in a sense what we do and how we express ourselves. We do bring work home with us and take us to work. The separation into compartmentalized realities robs us of the massive benefits of the paradox of appreciation and affiliation. These are the rewards of social effort whether work, family, volunteering, communities of faith, or any other social commitment and responsibility.

In the games we play of work, and family, and life we have an opportunity to not only have more fun and personal fulfillment but also to be more creative, productive and supportive of the others that are part of the game. It doesn't matter what role we or they play. Every person and every interaction is an opportunity to advance your personal and collective intention. It is all also practice enabling us to be able to play better in the future. Every expression reinforces who we are and who we want to be as we play together in our shared realities.

Chapter Seven Summary

- Social cognition is the active creation of a shared reality in a closer approximation to a situation/context.

- We are unique individual human beings who are social animals with shared realities based on our cultures.

- We think in patterns, are entertained by patterns, and fundamentally we are physical and mental patterns.

- We make up our realities as we play together in roles and games including all forms of work and other contexts.

- The neutral framework of paradox inherently reduces the noise, fear, and mistrust in social problem-solving.

- The framing of complex associations with paradox is fun, cognitively stimulating, and everyone can play.

Unity
Shared Meaning
Paradox
Together And Alone
Dependencies
Alignment And Commitment
Appreciation And Affiliation
Fear And Trust
Fun And Creativity
Teaching And Learning
Outcomes
Social Agreement And Aligned Intentions
Common Understanding

Chapter 8

The Way, The Paradox of Intention

In a world of infinite choices, possibly the most important ones we make are simply deciding what we want. In our discussion to this point, we have often reiterated the automatic nature of most of our thinking and doing behavior. Just like we might automatically respond to an environmental condition (trigger) with a habituated action (response) we also often take the same approach to choosing what we want.

I need to know two things to use the power of my intention intentionally; what I want and who I aspire to be. From a practical point of view this is extremely helpful for me, for groups and especially when there is conflict in choice or the definition of success in a certain situation. We can ask these questions and compare our alignment, talk through differences, and maybe find a common place of benefit. That benefit might be a compromise and, in many cases, it doesn't have to be especially when we try to maximize mutual benefit within agreed direction and values.

Unity

Intention

Paradox

What You Want to Do And Who You Want to Be

Dependencies

Desires And Needs
Individual And Social
Direction And Aspiration
Options And Choice
Unconscious And Purposive

Outcomes

Actions And Values
Direction

I believe that intention is the will that is done, the motive force. Most of us are unaware of how much power we really have to seek and apply our own will. I would maintain that if we can imagine a choice, our will allows us to make it. Now, you may say that things have consequences so they are not really choices and I bet you also can think of times where you and others escaped the consequences, got away with whatever it was and good and bad seemed bent - to your will. A practical assumption for consideration; we choose based on our will, we judge based on the outcomes at a specific time typically based on whether it advances our intention or not (and we apply our judgement frame to other people's choices too). Advances our intention is good, does not advance our intention is bad.

Intentions also reflect problem types and outcomes. For linear well-structured problems the intention are a form of As Good As It Gets within the required tolerance. For Ill-Structured problems and situations with more than one right answer, the intentions are an approximation of Close Enough.

In effect, as stated previously, we fix linear problems and balance paradoxical conditions. Balance in this case does not imply an increase of focus on one side of the paradox with a concurrent equal reduction of the other side like a conceptual teeter-totter. It means we focus the behaviors and outcomes of dependencies to result in what we want on both dimensions of intention; what we want and who we want to be. We also know that performance of any outcome can be any number of variations, possibly even an infinite number. Our goal is to describe what we want and then to manage within a range of acceptable performance and to make corrections when needed.

Our intentions lead to choices that we make that are consistent with what we want. Another consideration is what is available. In most cases there are a massive number of options more than we consider. While there may be many options there may also be many constraints. In effect, the constraints define a situational range for our options. While we looked at this paradox earlier as describing problem spaces, it also helps define the construct of choice.

Unity

Choice

Paradox

Opportunities And Constraints

Dependencies

Individual And Social Decisions

Imposed And Self-Selected

Automatic And Purposive

Desires And Expectations

Imagined And Experienced

Intention And Judgement

Outcomes

Options And Exclusions

Selections

We can use the Paradox Awareness Model to demonstrate how intention influences the dependencies and nature of the outcomes in a situation. Let's consider a few different intentions and how they might impact choosing a steak dinner.

Unity
> Steak Dinner

Paradox
> Preference And Options

Dependencies
> Product And Safety
> Cost And Availability
> Expertise And Method
> Individual And Social
> Taste And Selection
> Occasion And Expectations

Outcomes
> Cut And Temperature
> Order

The Paradox Awareness Model will be the same for each of three scenarios. Generally, unless there is a situational dependency that is more prominent, these models are stable for multiple different intentions. For simplicity in this instance, we can assume that the list of dependencies is sufficient to describe the important factors in the following three situations:

1. The bride's parents choosing menu options for a wedding reception dinner for 120 guests held at a country club.

An intention for this scenario could be: Provide a quality steak dinner option And Meet the expectations of guests and the Bride and Groom. The dependencies that are likely most prominent are Cost and Availability, and Occasion And

Expectations. The other dependencies are also important although likely would not be strong drivers in the choice. The opportunities are to have a wonderful and memorable reception and remain within a reasonable budget. The constrains are the budget, a limited single choice of cut and temperature for efficient service, along with the expectations of the couple and parents. A likely outcome choice might be medium temperature filets.

2. A retired teacher attending a regular monthly lunch with three old friends at their favorite chain steakhouse at the mall with a desire to spend less than twenty-five dollars.

An intention for this scenario might be: My favorite steak And Eating light because everyone is on a diet. The most prominent dependencies are Individual And Social, Cost And Availability, and Taste And Selection. The opportunity is to enjoy a favorite meal with good friends and pleasant social engagement. The constraints are limited menu options and smaller sized cuts and the taste preference of the retired teacher. A likely outcome might be the six-ounce sirloin well-done.

3. A first-time visitor to the Tokyo office of a company she just joined at a group business dinner at a highly regarded teppanyaki restaurant in Tokyo.

The intention in this case might be: Whatever others are having And Being polite and eating it no matter what. The prominent dependencies are Expertise And Method, Individual And Social, and Occasion And Expectations. The opportunities are to enjoy one of the best steaks in the world and build a relationship with important new business colleagues. The constraints are lack of choice and knowledge. The likely outcome is Chef's choice of multiple cuts prepared medium-rare.

Many times, we believe we must make a choice and it is only one thing or another. This leads us to think our choice is right and if someone else has picked some other choice then logically they must be wrong. How many are right and how many are wrong? None of them and all of them; it depends on what you want and the situation/context you are in. In our simplified examples we can see that the choice was essentially the same set of dependencies, but the intention drove the characteristics of the outcomes. These are simple examples and in other cases the options would be a much greater set of choices. Imagine a seasoned traveler off for a meal of their choice in Tokyo. They would have thousands of options and likely still consider only a small number.

Another aspect of the examples is that in each case there were a range of choices even within the limited scenarios. The wedding reception could have included sirloin, or strip steaks and maybe rare, medium, and well-done choices when indicated in advance by the guests. The Teacher could have had the small filet, or any other larger steak and taken half of it home. The businessperson could have studied the meal options in advance and politely asked to enjoy a specialty or indicated that they would very much like to try a little of everything.

In most cases there are many more options than are considered. We quickly bound the range in constraints even if they are easily overcome. As stated earlier, many times we don't even consider what our intentions are. We do what we have done before, we rely on others to choose, or we take the easiest or first choice that comes to mind. We just want to narrow it down and broaden it enough to work for us when it is important enough to take the extra effort. Important enough is also situational and it can be because of risk/reward, or being who we want to be (ethics/integrity/more fun or whatever we choose). It can also be because we are choosing for others, and we want to be as sure as possible to be in an acceptable range. For now, let's just assume that it is most useful to take the extra time when it is really important (however we personally define that at this point in time). I also believe this is quite useful when you are stuck, when there is conflict and when you want to achieve breakthrough results.

It may seem like the choices are endless and they are! Don't worry, you don't notice most of them. Suffice it to say though that in all situations there is a range of acceptable "right" choices and for those of us who are paid to choose, let's be OK with that and know that it is not static. We can also let ourselves relax a little because perfect is not the goal. We want to be reasonably close to what works for us. I'll add that I'm not telling you to be sloppy, if you know how something should be done, then do it but don't get too comfortable with surety.

There is a well-known story from the Tao about a father and his son. It is a favorite of mine and maybe you know it and if you don't, a quick paraphrased retelling. A farmer and his son awoke one day to find their horse missing. The neighbors all said. "What a terrible thing, your labor will be so much more difficult," and the farmer replied, "Maybe." The very next day, the horse returned with several other wild horses and the neighbors now said, "What great fortune, you are now wealthy with so many horses, what a great thing," and the farmer said, "Maybe." A few days later as the son was working to break one of the horses he was thrown off and broke his leg. Again, the neighbors came and said, "What a misfortune, your son is hurt, and these horses were a curse," and the father said "Maybe." Before the son could heal the army came through the village taking all the young men to war except the farmer's son because of his injury, the neighbors said, "How lucky you are that your son is spared," the father replied, "Maybe." Of course, this can go on indefinitely and reminds us that we can be sure that there is no easy surety and still we must choose.

Intention also applies to culture. The who we want to be aspect is not separate from what we want to accomplish. The value we intend to create and the social norms that accelerate our ability to do it. Common agreement becomes leverage for acceleration. Intention can be aspirational and practical. One of my favorite statements of intention is one I shared with a team early in my tenure as the group's leader. It was obvious that there was too little value being produced and too much work being done to achieve it. This problem of demand and capacity often becomes a discussion about resources and barriers. How many projects can be accomplished within the process by how many people in how much time. The paradoxical challenge I presented to the team was this intentional direction with the opportunity to think together to realize the performance promise:

> Create massively more value for less cost and effort in the best job you have ever had.

The issues were not demand management or resource availability. They were cultural, interpersonal, and managerial. The systems were not focused for performance, and it was not fun. Within a year it had completely changed, and the team did it themselves. Business units saw real value from the team's work, team members were highly regarded, throughput was much greater, and it was fun for all of us. A few guiding thoughts for creation and innovation with paradox.

> Anything that can be known, you can know.
> Anything that can imagined, can be real.
> We create our realities every day, this is normal.
> The path toward our intention is built from steps of approximation.

I'm a professional judge as are most people. I'm supposed to give students grades, choose from options for programs and projects, and determine if vendors have provided appropriate value. Maybe even to have an idea where my spouse and I should have lunch today. I must choose. I know it is inherently flawed by perspective and I still must move forward. It is important to know what is right and what is wrong and to be right and avoid being wrong and yet how can we know? We create structures and frameworks to help and rely on definitive sources and trusted opinions, and yet it still seems impossible to avoid a final "maybe."

Success and failure are the outcomes of choices; some we make intentionally, some automatically, some not at all, and some from others who also get to choose and yes some from random luck/disaster. These are a layer of complexity greater than choosing alone and are often the culmination of many choices. We can still judge them in the same way, through fidelity to our intentions. It is useful and important to realize that total success or total failure is rare. We might even change our intention during the process as we realize more about the situation, ourselves, and where the path is leading us.

I believe that most people are guided by good intentions most of the time and sometimes like the dog that finally catches it tail, we don't see the outcome clear enough to stop the chase. Choices lead to outcomes that based on our intentions we find to be successful or not (good or bad). Longer term, the performance of an aspect of a system may well be less important overall or even replaced by a new approach. It is useful to create directionally correct solutions and incremental approximations of Close Enough, maintaining fidelity to the situation and updating Close Enough as necessary. One last and very important point - if things don't go as we like - we can always choose again.

Chapter Eight Summary

- Intention describes what we want to accomplish and who we aspire to be.

- It is much easier to decide a course of actions from myriad options if you first establish your intention for the situation.

- Intentions are preferred direction, and none are right or wrong, it depends on the situation and person/group.

- Intention is a scalable alignment tool from the smallest choice to the long-term direction of an organization.

- Intention is another approximate aspect of human function and if it doesn't lead to where we want, we can choose again.

Unity

Intention

Paradox

What You Want to Do And Who You Want to Be

Dependencies

Desires And Needs
Individual And Social
Direction And Aspiration
Options And Choice
Unconscious And Purposive

Outcomes

Actions And Values
Direction

Chapter 9

New Worlds, The Paradox of Possibilities

I believe that the potential for creative expression is unlimited and the opportunity to do so is readily available. I also think that the application of paradoxical thinking can be a fundamental tool in this process. Reflecting what is and how we mentally perform provides a natural synergy that can be leveraged for massively more value. This includes the optimization of current systems and the fundamental reimagination of what is possible in new applications, models, relationships, and processes.

Maybe a lofty view and at the same time think about how many competitive advantages have been achieved by the novel combination of seemingly unrelated or opposite associations. A lodging empire without hotels, transportation companies who don't own fleets of cars, and the effective operation of businesses when hardly anyone came into the office. As the old saying goes, it's impossible until someone does it.

I would also maintain that there are two domains for this creative effort: in our expressed realities and within ourselves. We are the creators of our worlds through the models of meaning we apply and reinforce. Of course, our past experiences influence what we become as does our instinctual basis and it is still possible to achieve a closer approximation to our deeper aspirations. There is real potential to find greater peace of mind, satisfaction and clarity. It is also possible to express ourselves more fully in our contributions to social, physical, artistic, scientific, and labors of all kinds.

This may all sound a little pie in the sky – wait a minute, pie in the sky? Doesn't that sound like a great idea for airport kiosks? There could be fruit pies and savory pies in friendly self-service vending machine kiosks as a welcomed alternative to another sandwich or candy. A quick internet search reveals that a one-minute pie vending machine has already been developed so a prototype exists. I have seen fresh food vending machines now in airports, maybe.... I might not do anything with this idea beyond creating an example for you, and voilà now it's two possible creations: a pie vending machine and an example in this book. This is a bit playful, and it demonstrates just how easy this can be.

I really do think the potential for the application of paradoxical thinking and tools to improve and accelerate creativity is unlimited. For the purpose of our discussion, I'll limit it to a couple of areas and examples trusting that you will extend these things as you like. Of course, as you practice, they will also start to expand on their own as your mental models become more attuned with the possibilities. My focus will be on individual and social application with three aspects each: awareness, optimization, and novel expression. I know this is the tip of the iceberg and at the same time a useful conversation to get started.

Inner Space – Infinity Between Your Ears

Let's construct an awareness model for each of the levels of application. A word we can use for the unity of inner-space awareness is mindfulness which beyond techniques or programs means awareness of our thoughts. Next, we can choose a widely relevant paradox that supports this unity. I'll pick Attention And Detachment. Remember, I'm constructing meaning based on my opinion as an approximate example and you need not agree. If you like, try yourself and change anything that you like to reflect your understanding.

Mindfulness
Attention And Detachment

Now a few dependencies. For this example, some personal observations. This doesn't mean they are right, and they are close enough for me which is within the tolerances for the exercise.

Quiet And Open
Random And Specific
Ideas And Revelations
Ethereal And Flowing

And finally, what are the outcomes that result from this situation and concept? In my practice I would say Knowledge And Wonder. We have discussed this area in the previous chapters. The difference now is we are in metacognitive space. Thinking about thinking. There are many paths to this, from very rigorous to very simple. Sitting quietly and letting your mind wander is a good start. A paradox of this process is it doesn't have to be difficult to be very useful and simple practice is an approximation that may be close enough for our purposes.

It is also easy just to occasionally observe your responses and actions. What do the triggers feel like, what responses are generated? A few thought starters to become more attentive to your thoughts, a short stream of consciousness list to potentially choose from, a quick 50 or so:

Read, Talk, Write, Play, Contemplate, Daydream, Observe, Listen, Look Inside, Look Outside, Explore, Remember old Friends, Count your Curses and Blessings, Pretend, Take a Nap, Ask Yourself a Question before Bedtime, Wake up Early, Go for a Walk, Ride a bike, Take a Hot Bath, Walk in the Woods, Notice the Wind, Watch the Clouds, Put your Head Down on your Desk, Rake the Leaves, Watch a Fire, Sit on the Porch, Swing in a Swing, Meditate, Take a Drive, Float on Your Back, Canoe, Hum a Tune, Do Yoga, Go Fishing, Practice Tai Chi, Sit Quietly, Go to a Place of Worship between Services, Go to the Laundromat, Wash the Dishes, Float on a Raft, Tend the Garden, Smoke a Cigar, Vacuum, Sweep out the Garage, Look at Photographs, Ride a Bus, Get a Massage, Have your Hair Cut, Get your Nails Done, Get stopped at a Railroad, Saw some Wood, Put a Puzzle Together, Lie Down, Stare at a Candle, Pay Attention and then Relax, Brush your Hair, Sit on the Beach.

How many ways are there? I don't know but the more you do it, the more ways there are. I'm sure you have done most of these and while you were, for a moment or two your mind wandered, and you let it. Just ask yourself a question and allow yourself to appreciate the gift of your thoughts without judgement. Your automatic thoughts in your stream of consciousness are like a spring gently flowing, always there, refreshing you and giving life to consciousness. The mysterious paradox is that they are your thoughts and yet it seems as if they are formed by themselves.

Optimization: Deep and Wide

Enhanced Awareness

Recognition And Speed
Purposive And Automatic
Depth And Width
Specific And General
Common And Scalable

Broader Perspective And Unity Perception

How do you improve performance in anything? Practice with purpose. The intent of doing something well and doing it seamlessly. The opportunities for practice are again unlimited and you have been doing it while you read this book. Themes have been repeated and expanded, and simple models have been introduced. A guiding paradox for this effort is repetition and diversity. Do what you know and expand your thinking in new areas, to new associations and conflicts with your assumptions.

Mix it up, do something different, eat something different, go somewhere different, question yourself, question others, question authority, question dogma, question what your parents told you, question what you tell yourself. Think about the people who influenced you and saw in you things you didn't know where there, create a list of 20 paradoxes, explore humor, read sacred literature like they really meant what they said, talk to children, feed your automatic mind with seeds of the fruits you want to enjoy through books, videos, podcasts and talks with people you respect. Practice forgiveness of yourself and others, see them as pure expression of life energy just like you are. Follow yourself.

The paradoxical goal of mastery is effortless practice. This is not unfamiliar. Think of anything you have done so often that you no longer must think about it to do it like drive a car, brush your teeth, be comfortable at a cocktail party, play the piano, cast a reel, sing a song, recite poetry, and care about others. The way we naturally are, is not difficult to know. It is hiding in plain sight. We may have not thought about it, or maybe we thought it was more complex and difficult and that is also an illusion.

Novel Expression

New And Unique
Bespoke And Adapted
Giving And Receiving
Emerging And Making

Creation And Sharing

It is easy to think that an act of creation might be difficult or complex. Of course, that is a paradox as the most complex things are still based on simplicity. We are naturally creative, we do it all the time, and after all the work and practice we see that it was easy all along. Sometimes you might hear someone say something like, "I could never do that." I would argue that it happens on its own. We really don't have to make a lot of things happen; it is just how we are. We are natural creators, and it is play to us.

Think again back to childhood, making stories, building with blocks, drawing pictures, and making up a dance. That energy that drove you then is still there always ready at your command to share. The secret, if there is one, is that the path is what you enjoy and you like to share with others. Maybe that is telling a joke, singing karaoke, telling a story, writing a poem, taking a photo, arranging a room, and caring for others. Yes, paradoxical thinking can help you in this kind of expression and it can remind you that these things we do, and share are our highest expressions not because of their complexity but because of our intentions.

We do live in the world of duality, and we are prone to rapid judgement and rejection. We also inhabit the unities and have great capacity for forgiveness and contribution, they go together. This is not a fantasy or far off theoretical abstraction, it is our nature. We are two things and one thing, alone and together, positive and negative, and capable of being more of what we want and who we want to be. This part of the paradox of possibilities is the part we do alone and remember as was stated previously we are always alone and together. We can be physically separated but our realities are social, defined by our language, customs and strongly held beliefs. Our being is the result of the contributions made by our ancestors in our DNA, and the mental models and patterns shared by our caregivers, friends and loved ones. We are also the result of our own personal expressions and the those we share with others.

Social Application – Shared Vision

Paradox is the language of agreement. The use of paradoxical thinking in groups transforms conflict into opportunity and lays the foundation for common understanding of intention. It also leads to a closer approximation of an agreed shared reality. It is not deceitful and does not impose false realities. It does not create convenient false narratives imposed on others who still see the elephants in the room. There are no empty mantras conceived by others to be repeated until they think we have adopted their beliefs. It is simple and direct. It welcomes questions defenselessly and is not threatened by different opinions. While it feels like magic, it is not a trick.

Paradox has broad social application and scalable utility. It works in any situation where there are paradoxes and paradoxes are a universal condition. It can be accomplished with a degree of greater approximate value with little preparation and can be supported in important situations by practiced guidance. It also generally reduces fear predicated on unknown direction and cursory judgment. It is not the system or situation, and it supports accelerated performance in them. If something no longer fits, we don't need to destroy it, we can just let it go.

This approach is also playful and fun. Encouraging and accepting while maintaining and increasing performance. It is a source of massively more value, breakthroughs, impossible accomplishment, and the best place you have ever worked. It is at home in business, education, and any other social organization. A single person who understands the basics can create ripples of value and groups who do create waves of improvement.

Previously we discussed the creation of shared meaning with groups. In this section for the awareness level of social application, I'll take the point of view that you wish to use paradox in a group you lead or influence with some suggestions for your practice. Knowing some things yourself and applying what you learn as the occasions present themselves is the first step. Sharing your intentions using the model is also an easy step and introduces the concept in useful direction setting. You can also talk about the paradoxes you see and invite others to explore those with you.

Paradox can be integrated into many efforts from choosing priorities to evaluation of performance. Remember, if there are linear problems, use those tools. If there is a single right, as good as it gets or close enough answer, rely on those. If there is not, then there are paradox possibilities. Use the models and concepts and explore the possibilities with others.

A significant value at the basic awareness level is the recognition of multiple perspectives and influences. In Either/Or decision making it is often obvious that value has been neglected and conflicts unresolved. This is the classic Emperor's New Clothes story where leaders appear to be completely unaware of conditions. A paradox approach welcomes perspectives even those we disagree with or think inaccurate. Replacing good and bad ideas with preferred and intentionally aligned removes the risk for making contributions and increases the collective perspective. This leads to the possibility of clarity and alignment while also supporting positive relationships and engagement.

An additional advantage is the simplicity and comprehensiveness of the process. It is a succinct way to slow judgement when necessary. It is also a direct effort by the people who know and own the conflicts. It doesn't rely on distillation through instrumentation or rubrics possibly altering the situation through model effects. Additionally, the qualitative data is not numericized in a linear abstraction and therefore maintains a closer fidelity to observed meaning.

One of the aspects that I often see is that finally, common knowledge is commonly recognized. People see these conflicting conditions and the connections within them. The elephants in the room are no longer ignored and we don't pretend that everything is working just to avoid the conflict or effort. We also see the connections from our personal responsibility to organization outcomes and dependencies making deeper connections and increasing accountability. It is encouraging to see others, especially leaders, share a common reality and base choices and decisions on organizational and situational truths. This is also a great advantage for leaders in engaging the power of social cognition, identifying the opportunities for delegating choices, and increase accuracy and efficiency.

Optimization: Deep and Wide

Enhanced Awareness

Recognition And Speed
Purposive And Automatic
Depth And Width
Specific And General
Common And Scalable

Broader Perspective And Unity Perception

This level of use is where Paradoxical Inquiry® comes in. it can be used to optimize systems, process, and outcomes and extend to novel application. The additional structure is useful especially in important situations as judged by those involved and their organizations. There are also absolute advantages from using expert guided practice. If this option is not available as described in Chapter Five an approximate model can be accomplished by anyone using the simple questions below.

- Where am I? (My condition/context)

- What do I want? (My intention)

- What are the contextual and social conditions that must also be considered?

- Where is the possible agreement and synergy?

- What is the outcome we collectively desire?

- What would we nudge to move toward this new state?

There are some challenges in doing this yourself. The first is that with groups you already know, there is a frame of reference for how you work together that will be a naturally applied making it more difficult to represent a new way. A second challenge is maintaining the neutral perspective even to the point of not saying things like, "That looks good." The third challenge is avoiding numeration of the data and findings. We are so used to this process of assigning numbers to things that it is second nature. The most important limitation is the risk of not being a peer thinker in the process and appearing to maintain conceptual authority and instead of contributing what they think, teams contribute what they think you want to hear. It is a bit challenging to juggle all the balls with one foot in the process and the other guiding it. Of course, it is still an approximation and if there are limitations in getting support, it is as good as it gets for now.

There is wide utility for the methodology from an annual organization performance review, merger and acquisition integration, specific conflict resolution, and convening around a single issue or opportunity. I have observed several different motivations/intents for the process with consistent results; clarity of meaning and options for action And improved communication, engagement and team affiliation.

Novel Expression

New And Unique
Bespoke And Adapted
Giving And Receiving
Emerging And Making

Creation And Sharing

There is so much possibility for novel creativity using paradox. This can range from an aspirational paradox like the massively more value statement, to new product development and breakthrough operations approaches. This is the space of impossible achievement and significant competitive advantage.

Generally speaking, there are three levels of performance paradoxes: Strategic, Operational, and Enabling. These could also be described as purpose, processes and supporting systems. All organizations have these, and few realize competitive advantage across all three. Another area of Either/Or, what do we choose to be really good at and what do we accept to be table stakes and non-differentiating effort. They are all opportunities for acceleration and why not? We do them anyway, and have already committed to the cost and effort. Real competitive advantage appears to me like the model below.

Competitive Advantage
Market Recognition And Exceptional Performance

Leverage And Foresight
Engagement And Affiliation
Approximate And Opportunistic
Competition And Collaboration

Massive Value And less Cost and Effort
Preeminence

An interesting exercise for any organization would be to create a current state model and future performance aspiration. This is simple, pretty easy to do, and in my opinion, much more tangible and practical that most strategic planning artifacts like visions, missions, and values. When using those statements, we can also describe our intentions for each aspect and create seamless alignment.

Remember these are fractal models and can be worked further down and serve as a simple performance evaluation model. What I have showed you is some generic models based on my experience and perspective. There is absolute value in building these together as a team as alignment and engagement go along with direction and outcomes. Every aspect has the potential for competitive advantage. A few examples of common areas for attention at each level:

Strategic:
Business analytics, internal and competitive
Mergers and acquisitions
Transformations and turn-arounds
Simulations and systems dynamics
Investment and risk management

Operational:
Planning and execution
Organization and fulfillment
Research and development
Supply chain management
Marketing and sales

Enabling
Organization effectiveness
Policy, Process, and procedure
Selection, roles, and responsibilities
Engagement and reward
Evaluation and controls

This can also be done for any type of organizations at any level of scale. Focus for attention comes from both performance degradation/issues and from a constant attentiveness to leverage and synergy. This is the tip of the iceberg.

Chapter Nine Summary

· Paradoxical thinking can be a foundational tool in creativity for us individually and within our social contexts.

· There are three levels of application and leverage: Awareness, Optimization, and Novel Expression.

· The opportunities for practice are unlimited.

· The paradoxical goal of mastery is effortless practice.

· Paradox can be integrated into many efforts from choosing priorities to evaluation of performance.

· The models and components of Paradoxical Inquiry® can be used to support individual and team performance.

· Guided use of the approach is recommended, and an approximate value can be obtained by anyone informally.

· There are three levels of performance paradoxes: Strategic, Operational, and Enabling, all can provide competitive advantage.

Unity

Possibilities

Paradox

Renewal And Release

Dependencies

Aspiration And Creativity

Extension And Expansion

Paradox And Unity

Outcomes

Optimize And Reimagine

Advantage

Chapter 10

Two Roads in a Snowy Woods, The Paradox of Choice

Few of us live our lives with intention with good reason. How can we know? What do we really control and what is just the flow of unknown causes? Do our choices even matter in the end? We know the ultimate answer is maybe, and also yes and no. We can't know the paths we didn't take even though sometimes we spend a lot of time on speculating on lost opportunities or better lives. Has it all been good or bad?

I would maintain that the judgment of the value of our experience is up to us. Reality is What Is independent of that opinion although we allow it to cloud our view. I think we have two options if we want to change that view; we can change our minds and we can change the situation. Both can be difficult and easy, scarry and exciting, and it will happen no matter what. Our lived experience has shown us that change is constant and also that at our core we seem to have always been the same. I am the little boy who will be an old man, and this is my constant, to me a comforting recognition of self.

This is not some mysterious metaphysical observation. It is our foundational condition and where we can start from in doing what we want to do and being who we want to be. Consider that our core self is no different based on what we do, it is always the same. Our judgments about our actions, beliefs, and situation don't change reality either although we allow the illusion to persist as if it did.

Our perceived realities are what we think they are. Of course, we do not choose alone and sometimes others impose their wills upon us. Even when we have absolutely no control over our environments and situations, we still can choose what our experience means to us and ultimately how we will carry this Now into our futures.

We have unlimited potential and power to shape our understanding and create our realities. This power is magnified when we do it together. In the end, choice is about change. All choices are an effort to change our realities, from the very simple change of satisfying our hunger with lunch to changing the direction and performance in a large organization. The collective understanding of a new reality is an automatic continuous process and one we can further leverage with intention.

Unity

               Choice

Paradox

             Individual And Social Decisions

Dependencies

                Imposed And Self-Selected

                Desires And Expectations

                Imagined And Experienced

                Intention And Judgement

Outcomes

                Options And Selections

                 Decisions

Choice also includes judgement. Judgement is fraught with layers of risk. The impacts of poor choices can be financial, social, and even physical danger. This is extremely important and not left completely to our intellectual process. It can be very high stakes in our jobs where we are supposed to make the right choices, with our families and social groups, and in our individual behavior as judged by ourselves and others.

No matter what systems of thought and guidance for behavior we accept and are influenced by, we still are the ultimate judges, and that judgment is based on our intention even if we are not aware of it. It comes back to what we want and who we want to be. I believe that an understanding of paradox empowers us to make choices more consistent with our intentions and to be able to do that more effectively. Paradox can also help us to derive additional practical value in unlimited ways. I would like to introduce three more paradoxes related to judgement for your consideration. The three unities and paradoxes are related to choices in the past, present, and future.

Past
Forgiveness And Acceptance

Present
Giving And Receiving

Future
Flexibility And Approximation

I believe these concepts are accelerators toward intention and value creation. They are practical elements of wisdom and available to all of us to use. I have found them to be essential ingredients in fulfilling my intentions as a leader and the accomplishment of personal core intentions. With each, we will start with my interpretation of the Awareness Model.

Unity
>						Past
Paradox
>						Forgiveness And Acceptance
Dependencies
>						Events And Memories
>						Willingness And Tolerance
>						Grievance And Continuity
Outcomes
>						Release And Resolution
>						Reconciliation

A paradox of forgiveness is that it is directed at others and is about you. It is a practical matter of resolving a conflict in the past with your current intention. It does not require the participation of others or any pronouncement or other action directed to a person who you believe is responsible for hurting you. It is not about an offense or offender in this sense, it is only about you and your achievement of your intentions.

Our conceived past is a story of success and failure, hurt and healing, and accomplishments and mistakes. It is over and it still may not be resolved. The conflict inherent in the past is that in many instances we did not get what we wanted or were impeded from realizing who we wanted to be. This happens all the time as we interact with others who also have intentions, from family members to all forms of social groups and social patterns of morality, control, and ultimately meaning.

There is no question that trauma, deprivation, and abuse can have lifelong negative effects. This book is not intended as a substitute for profession medical and psychological help and that is an important path particularly in cases where the past impedes your realization of your intentions and the accomplishment of your best life. Often it is useful to have help with deep seated issues to achieve resolution and release.

I have been a manger in organizations for many years with the responsibility for organization, individual, and team performance and the performance of the groups I directly lead. This has included increasing levels of responsibility and several new jobs and companies. In almost every experience soon after I have been hired or promoted, I've been advised to fire someone for prior poor performance. Generally, I've responded to these statements with the question, "If you knew this needed to be done, why didn't you do it before I got here?"

In all of these cases I did not fire the person and instead gave them direction with a simple paradoxical approach, appropriate expectations and important work. Now of course I had no prior grievance to be associated with the person. My observation has been that for whatever reason the person had lost the confidence of their team and leader and instead of addressing the issue the leader and team choose to marginalize them. This created a self-fulfilling prophecy as the lack of trust resulted in less valued performance. The initial issue may have been the employee's, but the ongoing issue was the leader's performance. It was the leader's job to remediate the performance or separate the employee. In almost every case the marginalized employee became a valued team member.

I believe organizational and individual forgiveness is a key to reconciling past mistakes with current conditions. That doesn't mean overlooking current poor behavior. It is clearing the mental debris of past mistakes through acceptance of the impact of the grievance and breaking the association with our current state. This applies to our perceptions of other's failures as well as our own mistakes. We judge others through our own expectations and beliefs, and these may be in complete error and the accused offender may not care at all. Our judgements of others are always reflections of ourselves and the hurt we feel is self-imposed beyond the original offense as we allow a memory to continue to cause us pain.

Effectively, holding onto grievance is a paradox of not getting what we want in a situation that is no longer there. We can blame ourselves and others and it won't help now. Similarly, when we have wronged someone and struggle with guilt, we may be able to make restitution, but we can't be relieved of our mental burden by anyone else no matter what their response. We must forgive ourselves and understand that no matter how bad a behavior or error was, it is no longer here. Our forgiveness intent includes what we want to do about our past and who we want to be to ourselves and others. I know this can be difficult and healing starts with the recognition that it is our choice.

A provocative concept for consideration: All past human effort has failed to some extent as will all future human effort. A major contributing factor to this failure is us; what we think, what we do, what we believe, and the truth that we thought we found. Sometimes it is important and sometimes it doesn't matter and most times we don't know which. This is what I think freezes and scares us. We don't want to fail. We want to be right, to be alright, to be respected, to be happy, and to be safe. Now, don't despair, this is the nature of creativity. The universe doesn't create to be right, profitable, or a good idea. It just creates in every direction and possibility.

Let's avoid the trap of attributed failure. We see it all the time. In isolation events can be judged good and bad, and successful or not. A favorite (and really easy) means of criticism is to point out those failings in others. This gives us the power to reject their ideas, proving our superiority and greater value along the way. What we see is a moment in a continuity that we don't know where it came from or where it is going. Let's try to understand intent, to encourage each other and when things don't work, to choose/try again. Let's continue to search for right being as we try to be right, applying the simple measure of intent: To accomplish our goals and be who we aspire to be as we practice the way together.

When we reflect on the past and consider our individual and social experiences, we can see that we have been on a shared path of expression. Expression is the reality we create for ourselves and share with others. It is What Is and it is a great paradox. We don't have to do anything, and we can do everything. We take guidance from our collective wisdom, judgements of our experiences, sacred beliefs, and systems of thought. We may align with anything we choose or nothing at all. We are always together and always alone, and ultimately, we get to decide what it all means.

Unity

          Present

Paradox

          Giving and Receiving

Dependencies

          Win/Lose And Win/Win
          Leverage And Acceleration
          Creation And Destruction
          Appreciation And Recognition

Outcomes

          Contribution And Benefit
          Mutual Value

I was once in a classroom in a factory in the middle of the night with a group of production employees in my role as a new senior manager explaining and trying to engage them in changes that were occurring where we worked. The company had just gone through a sale with a significant change in philosophy and direction and people were concerned and afraid. As we talked about what was happening and where we were going one of the participants said in an aggressive fashion, "In the end we are all just going to die!" My reply was, "You're right, what are you going to do between now and then?"

I remember when I was a little boy, I loved to climb a tree in our yard and enjoy the wind in the leaves and on me. I know that the me who enjoyed that experience still does, and the Now from then is still my Now. Since then, I have had great adventures. I have played in tragedies and comedies. I have explored the world around me and within me. I have had play-mates who loved me and some not so much.

I have chased desires and made mistakes. I have hurt others and been selfish. I have also shared and healed and been amazed. I am always there for me, and I know I always will be. I also know that I will always share that Now with others and collectively it is the same Now for all of us.

Sometimes it is fun to pretend to play alone and the most fun has been the times I played together with others as we created our realities of families, friendships, work, and loved ones. In these games we take and give, share and steal, fight and cooperate. Sometimes we argue about the rules, some-times I win and sometimes I lose. I share this with you and the view through the paradox lens as an encouragement, as appreciation, and as another possibility for framing our games both those we play by ourselves and when we involve others. I have witnessed the value, appreciation, and fun this brings. I know that it reduces confusion, fear and doubt and even the most basic recognition of Both/And is transformative. It is an option available to you, Now.

One of my favorite sayings is, "Everyone works for me, and I work for everyone." Occasionally when I say this people respond that I should not think of anyone working for me and I understand the sentiment. I agree that we work with each other and still I maintain that I absolutely receive value from the effort of others. I do my best to do the same. The point I want to make is this – the world, universe, everyone, is poten-tially able to help you and you can do the exact same thing and no matter what – we all give, and we all take.

In business, and in life in general, it appears that there are limits to resources, money, attention, value, everything. Maybe so and maybe not. In workshops, I like to ask people to think about a time they did something for someone for free. Always, every person can recall an example. When I ask why they did it, they say because someone needed them, they loved them, they asked, it seemed like the right thing to do, or maybe it was a random act of kindness. I then tell them that we have established that they are all willing to work for free, and maybe all I need to do is figure out what would motivate them to help me. Now I also tell them that several years ago I adopted the bias of saying yes when asked to help and I generally do. It has been one of my favorite personal choices.

One aspect that is useful in practice is to separate what we have from what we can give. Surely, we can give of our possessions and still the inventory of value we can share is massively more than what we own. So how do we give more than we have? Let's focus on another paradox that applies to the abundance of the universe and ourselves – things that we give that we also keep. This is a cool paradox; I have things I can give away and still have? Of course, we do and when we give these things, they are often magnified for us too, so much so that we might just think we got more than we gave. A few simple examples of these: Encouragement, Appreciation, Listening, Laughter, Hope, Wisdom, and Love.

Another favorite paradox for me is Give What You Want. It might not be exactly in the form of the final desire, and it is all just an approximation anyway. We inherently are creating all the time, why not try to consistent with your intentions? Why not start? With practice we build patience for the lack of total specificity. We also do this with intellectual arrogance, blind faith, and our confidence in ourselves. As nothing we do is really in isolation from other events or situations, it all melds together in the end as we rush headlong into the future.

It is not important to agree. Due to the infinite variety of experience and perception while we can hear the same words, they don't represent the same story. That is OK, the telling is the start. We see together even if we don't agree on what it is we are looking at. That is our initial place of agreement. That is how we can practically use paradox to help people and organizations and ourselves. I could not have predicted the path of my life at any point in it and yet I felt that in some way I controlled it. I don't know what the future holds either and I expect to go there for a while. I make plans and have intention and when I'm thoughtful I'm patient with myself and the unwinding of my road.

As the Robert Frost poem reminds us, we can't know the paths we didn't take and that is ok. We choose and explore in the direction we want or feel we must. The scenery may change and yet the continuity is that I'm still the traveler. I look forward to the journey and sharing the experience with those who go with me and that I'll meet along the way. My map is my intention, and I can change that as I go. No matter what, I know I will be surprised. I know I will have fun, and I know I will face challenges that I would have avoided if I knew what they would be and still I value those experiences as well.

Unity
           Future
Paradox
           Flexibility And Approximation
Dependencies
           Explore And Adjust
           Succeed And Fail
           Confidence And Doubt
Outcomes
           Continuity And Change
           Experience

Paradoxes have many dimensions, and our understanding of situations, experience, players, and perceptions help us form these mental structures. As we multiply perception by the number of persons who bring their unique perspectives it is amazing that we find agreement at all, and still we do. An agreement with built-in flexibility because it is exactly non-exact. I know that sounds ridiculous and it works. It works to be directionally aligned and for the most important aspects of a situation have at least general agreement on what they are, what influences them, how we might manipulate them for improvement, and be able to correct course when needed.

An important aspect of this directional framing is that it is not too specific. Another paradox, fuzzy goals? Not exactly and yes. What I have learned is that driving to a too specifically defined outcome or metric may inadvertently cap value for yourself and others. That's interesting, we create expectations and measures to guide us, but we should not let them drive us. Leverage comes from synergy and the amount and value of synergy depends on mutual goodwill and effort; therefore, I can't define it in advance. I can't make anyone else benefit beyond their expectations including myself, we must do that together and, in my experience, if we do, there it is. We are not looking for the absolute, single universal answer. We want to know what to do now knowing full well that things will change.

This reveals a possibly uncomfortable paradox; our solutions are right until they are wrong. So, what is the shelf life of a thoughtful selection of choices? As long as it works for us. Another way to think about this is that things get done for now and we should expect to do them again when the context/situation changes. The more important something is the more attention we should pay to it and the more we need to do something when it no longer works.

Chapter Ten Summary

· Our self is our source of continuity.

· Choice is influenced by the type of decision, decision makers, criticality, and options with the potential to choose again.

· Organizational and individual forgiveness is a key to reconciling past mistakes with current conditions.

· We can't know the paths we didn't take. We choose and explore in the direction we want, always in the Now.

· We can't predict the future and driving to a too specifically defined outcome may inadvertently cap value.

· The future includes a directionally correct approximate model.

Unity
Choice
Paradox
Individual And Social Decisions

Dependencies
Imposed And Self-Selected
Automatic And Purposive
Desires And Expectations
Imagined And Experienced
Intention And Judgement
Outcomes
Options And Selections
Decisions

Chapter 11

Paradoxical Inquiry, The Paradox of Reasoning

Paradoxical inquiry defined: Paradoxical inquiry is a process for revealing, describing, evaluating, and intervening in paradoxical conditions.

In a general sense paradoxical inquiry would be anything related to thinking about paradox, looking for them, and applying methods to benefit from these phenomena. This is an ancient art and recent science. The fundamental tools that have been used for recorded history are those of philosophy and logic. These are still useful and enlightening. More specifically, Paradoxical Inquiry® defined as a model and type of disciplined inquiry is a process that results in clarity and choice. It takes us from, "What is going on?" to "What do we want to do about it?" As with any model it has great potential and some limitations. The ultimate goal is to reach a closer approximation of our intentions and whenever possible, to do that together.

There are two general sets of paradoxical meaning making tools; those directly described as paradox interventions and a much larger set of tools that are based on a paradoxical premise. Paradox interventions include paradox specific tools like a Polarity Map® (2013, Polarity Partnerships LLC). The much larger set of tools with a foundational premise in paradox include Is and Is/Not, As/Is and To/Be, SWOT, Force Field Analysis, Four and Nine Block Diagrams, and Appreciative Inquiry (2005, Cooperrider and Whitney) to name a few.

A significant difference between Paradoxical Inquiry® and the other tools is that most of them are extensions of the Good/Bad paradigm and interject immediate judgement into the process. For example, a SWOT (Strengths, Weaknesses, Opportunities, and Threats) analysis sorts characteristics as strengths or weaknesses, essentially currently good and bad things, and opportunities and threats, projected good and bad things. When we start with a directional bias it might be a more rapid process but it treats the aspects in isolation as if they are only one thing or the other. If you have done these before the thought may have occurred to you that some items could be in both boxes. This is not to say there isn't utility and that depends on the intention of the group. The approach used in all box sorting methods provides some more information while also being a predetermined forced fit.

Appreciative Inquiry (AI) developed by David Cooperrider and others and widely used in organization development is in some respects a response to deficit-based thinking. Most problem solving is deficit focused, essentially asking the question, "What is wrong?" Appreciative Inquiry and similar strengths-based approaches are positively biased asking the question, "What is right?" Thinking paradoxically, we can see that these are two sides of a unity that we described previously – What Is. The exclusion of either side of this coin limits the understanding of both the other side and the unity represented.

While certainly an improvement over simple deficit thinking alone there is another aspect of AI and similar methods that sounds logical and mimics the error of benchmarking. That is using previous successful experience to create potential current solution options. Thinking about a previous success in a similar situation is not the current situation. This may sound like splitting hairs and fidelity to reality is a foundational aspect of improved problem solving and understanding. As stated previously meaning is based on context/situation and every step away introduces error in understanding.

Problems are context dependent. I conducted an experiment with expert engineers in electronics representing design, manufacturing, and repair work. The experts solved the problems that were representative of their typical work but struggled with simple faults from the other perspectives. They knew the system, the components, and had all of the tools necessary including the same processes to troubleshoot but started with their usual mindsets and predetermined assumptions even though they did not know what kinds of faults to expect. They recognized the symptoms but couldn't solve the problems. Generally, they assumed aspects of the situation and did not go back to question their initial mental models. Their success was limited by a framing bias.

In both deficit-based and positivistic, or strengths-based, approaches judgement is introduced as a foundation aspect early in the process. These are fundamentally well-structured linear problem-solving concepts and techniques that have been applied to non-linear and ill-structure problems. This is not unusual given a general bias to try to fix any issue independent of problem type and a reliance on those techniques in many problem-solving tools. Paradoxical Inquiry is a fundamentally different approach with a neutral and broader perspective. The positive aspect in the approach is the refreshing and energizing way people work together.

Another set of tools that are a close fit for paradox come from the practice of mediation and these tools are related to the direction, conduct, and conflict within and during an inquiry session. In a sense, Paradoxical Inquiry® can be described as a form of whole group mediation. The facilitator or convener is encouraging and supportive while remaining neutral even avoiding affirmation or criticism of ideas. The guidance through the process is not based on a teacher who already knows the right answer. What the answers will be is always up to the groups. It is their issue, and their intention drives where it will ultimately lead. It is easy to fall into Teacher/Student or Facilitator/Participant personas as these are the typical contextual roles. This is a subtle art and best accomplished by someone without a stake in the outcome who can adopt as much as possible a neutral perspective.

The process requires a commitment from leaders to participate as peers with subordinates. The sessions are structured so that everyone on all of the teams is a contributor and for the period of the process engaged in thinking together. It is a moment of acceleration among people. It is energizing and fun. It doesn't mean they particularly agree, or even understand. It is closer to collectively being open to listening without rapid or cursory judgement.

When we structure our work in paradox, we don't discuss such things (as then it becomes some external thing) and we do create a context that accomplishes this. It is a continuous effort that creates the power of shared minds. We share realities to find what we collectively understand, think, and feel. The connection is to a deeper self as we allow ourselves to share and at the same time a deeper appreciation of others. People who attend these workshops say something is different. It is better and while it feels that way it is also elusive. It works and they are not sure exactly why. You can't make people do this and most people really want to.

The essential question asked and answered in Paradoxical Inquiry® is What is and What do you want? It might be driven by an issue, change, possibility, or even curiosity. The basis is a conflict and that can be any type or form. The outcomes might be performance improvement in a system, alignment of teams around direction, or breakthrough possibilities establishing a path toward greater success. It also inherently improves teamwork, relationships, communication, and appreciation. It helps teams think and it changes the way they do. The process is a bridge between confusion and connection that results in a renewed sense of opportunity, affiliation, and value.

Unity

        Paradoxical Inquiry®

Paradox

        Conflict And Opportunity

Dependencies

        Individual And Team
        Opinions And Perspectives
        Reality And Options
        What Is And What you Want

Outcomes

        Realization And Renewal
        Shared Direction

Paradoxical Inquiry® Phases - Reveal, Reimagine, Refine, and Renew

These are not just steps or a recipe, they are what happens when we think together. While they are a framing order for the activity, they are also concurrent, emergent, and underlying in each phase. This basic process also occurs in a context of convening that promotes thinking together within a structure but not strongly driven by timed milestones or close facilitative/instructional management. It includes an experiential element with a physical example of the concepts supporting a heart, head, and hands full-person experience to reinforce concepts and strengthen connections.

The process starts with an interest to explore the paradoxes within situations. It could be around a single topic or multiple areas/issues. It might be predicated on a specific conflict that has gone unresolved or an effort to look for even stronger performance in already well performing teams. It works in any situation where there are paradoxes and a desire to reach a more preferred close enough or as good as it gets condition.

Phase One: Reveal

In the first phase of the process, teams describe an intention for the Inquiry, build an Awareness Model, explore connections to a bigger picture, and craft a description of the current As-Is state of What Is in the situation. The process and outcomes can be described by the model below:

Unity

Reveal

Paradox

Situation And Outcomes

Dependencies

Unity And Paradox

Characteristics And Dependencies

Intention And Outcomes

Opinions And Perspectives

Is And Is Not

Outcomes

Understanding And Alignment

Shared Reality

In the first part of the process, the paradox or paradoxes of interest are identified. The goal is to identify possibilities for inquiry and not to immediately summarize or limit the effort. A caution is not to change the meaning through simplification or summary with other concepts, at least not immediately. The process is scalable from single groups to large organizational whole-structures. The criteria for inclusion in the pool of contributors is a first-hand knowledge of the situation and responsibility for leading, managing and/or executing the effort.

These are not done anonymously as the person who suggests the paradox will be critical in describing the situational characteristics and nature of the current conflict. An advanced effort to collect the paradoxes reduces social acceptability influences that might result in deferring to authority or what may appear to be socially acceptable instead of an authentic contribution. Groups are formed based on topic clusters. Preferable team sizes should be between four and seven. The teams can be mixed levels of authority and perspective, and no one is named to lead groups.

The goal is to build an As/Is representation of the paradox/conflict. Team members share perspectives and build a Paradoxical Inquiry Awareness Model. The initial effort is to name the unity. This is looking at the common aspect of the seemingly opposite or unrelated elements. This answers the question, "What is the overall process or condition?" It also makes it plain that the two aspects are the source not only of issues but also synergies and solutions. This can be a serious gestalt opportunity and it is helpful to reinforce that we are not working from the either/or perspective but truly from a both/and point of view. The right answer does not come from a facilitator, it comes from the group and while they are working through this, they are reframing how they look at the issue together in social cognition space.

Next the teams describe the outcomes from the paradox pair. The performance of the outcomes paradox is a factor of the dependency paradoxes that are prominent influences contributing to the choices in the construct. Essentially, the question is "What does the outcome quality depend on for this unity and paradox pair?" There can be many of these and many layers of related meaning. The goal is to discover what the groups think are the major drivers. not a long or exhaustive list. It should be what they think has the greatest impact, not an aspirational or theoretical answer but their experience and awareness in the current state.

The paradox that the individuals are struggling with is part of a complex system of interdependent concepts and choices that is producing an unwanted, confusing, or unexpected outcome result. It is also based on, and contributes to, other systems and choices. Teams explore the systems that support and shape the dependencies and those that rely on the outcomes as dependencies in those systems. Effectively answering the paradoxical question, "what does this depend on and what depends on this?"

At the end of the this first phase an approximate view of the current state has been created. This includes an Awareness Model including the unity, the presenting paradox, and the agreed prominent dependencies that contribute to the performance and the outcomes. It also includes a broader view of the context from the dependencies and the contributions made by the outcomes. The total information derived in this phase is described in a presentation of As/Is. These are representations of a newly shared social reality. Previously, these may have been topics of conversation and possibly not. As they are revealed and agreed upon, the power of social cognition creates a clearer perspective, and the process establishes a shared sense of meaning and connection.

These sessions are a continuous relationship and team building effort. Generally, this is subtle, and it is also occasionally the complete focus. Reflecting on play reminds us of the importance of a little frivolity and the connections it makes. Exploring and play are designed in and are closely linked to the physical paradoxes and environments used as object lessons. I would recommend at the end of phase one to leave the workshop environment, explore something new and unique, enjoy a meal, and have some fun. This refreshes everyone and allows some time to settle and reconsider the initial work.

Phase Two: Reimagine

How do you benefit as much as possible from everything you do? What is possible and what seems impossible now? The potential outcome states are infinite. What would a directionally correct good enough or as good as it gets look like? Phase Two of the model describes the To-Be state that will deliver desired outcomes and related intentions to guide the process.

Unity
Reimagine
Paradox
Intentions and Possibilities

Dependencies
Win/Win And Win/Win/Win/Win
Aspiration And Synergy
Leverage And Benefit
Close Enough And As Good as it Gets
Outcomes
Options and Direction
Choices

In imagining possibilities, the goal is to create a deep and wide view. Everyone considers and contributes to a rich variety of possibilities to reshape the outcomes. The essential question is, "What could be different for the outcomes of this unity/paradox that would enable a closer approximation to Close Enough and leverage possibility synergies for breakthrough value and optimized systems?"

Results are both practical and aspirational. No effort should be made to describe how the possibilities are realized as in a solution/project. Teams are encouraged to create a large set for consideration. Possibilities typically would be described as one or a few words at most. A few questions serve as thought starters for possibility creation from both sides of the outcomes.

- What seems impossible that would be breakthrough value if someone could figure it out?

- What adds massively more value with less cost and effort?

- What would support the best job you ever had?

- What are possible synergies for improved system outcomes?

The next step is to identify the possibilities in three general categories for both sides of the outcomes paradox (six total sets of options):

Breakthrough Advantage - This level of revised outcomes would result in competitive advantage, paradigm shift, and generally unimagined possibility.

As Good As It Gets - These are options at the limits of what is considered possible. They are feasible and might represent a significant improvement in current performance.

Close Enough - This category represents possibilities that describe effective performance and remediate issues such that they outcomes are no longer a barrier or hindrance. They are viable alternatives to the current state.

The teams write intention statements for each of the three levels incorporating the possibilities. The intention statements include elements of both what we want to do, and who we want to be for the Outcome Unity.

Phase Three - Refine

In the refine phase teams share their ideas and models with others to expand perspectives and get feedback. They also refine the Awareness Model and consider how the dependencies will need to change in order to support the new statement of outcome intentions. The initial effort is a peer review presentation and feedback session. In workshops with multiple groups this can be accomplished by pairing two small groups or other division. Another similar peer review is accomplished at the end of the phase.

Unity

Refine

Paradox

Tell And Ask

Dependencies

Constraints And Opportunity
Engage And Appreciate
Reality And Perspectives
Intention And Options

Outcomes

Understanding And Improvement
Enhancement

What is changed to modify the paradox and outcomes to a desired state? Awareness of the system, social agreement on performance and the need for modification, and the dependencies in the system. This is a very interesting aspect of the awareness model and concept of paradox as described by this approach. The paradoxes, unities, and outcomes generally remain the same. Of course, the performance of the outcomes is variable and reflects the performance within the dependencies. In some cases, there may be the need to add a discovered dependency that has a prominent influence on the outcomes that was not previously identified or recognized.

This is an extremely powerful point of view and one with unlimited possibilities. As I have described these models over many examples, I have provided my characterization of what the prominent dependencies are in each situation or concept. I'm sure I'm approximately correct, and in any specific application and context, they may be different. Let's look at an awareness model for dependencies:

Unity

Dependencies

Paradox

Latent And Prominent

Dependencies

Awareness And Attention
Assumed And Prescribed
Beliefs And Biases
Tangible And Intangible
Causal And Creative
Recognized And Unknown

Outcomes

Outcomes And Assumptions
Performance

Three processes are applied to the dependencies. The first is to identify any dependencies that will be more prominent in influencing the performance that are not included on the list and adding them. The second is to accomplish a From-To analysis to describe how the current performance of each dependency will need to change in order to deliver the new intention including overcoming potential constraints. The third effort is to identify recommendations for changes based on the analysis.

The change recommendations are categorized as immediate and longer term. Immediate changes would be those that are simple, have wide agreement, and can be easily implemented. Longer term changes may be more complex, costly, and higher risk. They may require additional input and broader involvement or other changes to occur first. It is not a process to create a long list of action items. It is to adjust to a closer approximation of intentions. It may be that working through the process was a sufficient intervention in itself. It might be a choice to do nothing if there is little value to be gained or the timing isn't yet right.

Choices can be anything that effects a directionally appropriate change in the system. The best candidates are likely the most obvious choices, remembering that you can always choose again as preferred. A nudge approach recognizes that in a complex system a relatively minor change might be amplified in its interactions with other elements. If a process is not continuous, it will also take a period of time to see differences. In any event, focusing on one or two directional momentum changers limits risk and isolates causality/impacts. At the end of the phase another peer review based on the same approach as earlier is accomplished. This feedback is considered, and modifications made to the models for a whole-group peer review at the beginning of the final phase.

Phase Four - Renew

This phase starts with a whole-group peer review to increase the feedback perspectives and gain support for the recommended changes. The groups present the As-Is and To-Be using the Awareness Model, system connections, possibility intentions, and recommendations for immediate action approvals and awareness of potential longer-term changes. The phase extends into actions for modification and monitoring of the paradox performance and support for the changes and new performance after the workshop.

Unity

                    Renew

Paradox

                Stability And Change

Dependencies

                  Direction And Flexibility
               Leverage And Acceleration
               Engagement And Affiliation
             Inspiration And Approximation

Outcomes

               Intention And Action
                  Enhancement

During the whole group review, common areas for change may be identified as dependencies underly multiple concepts/constructs and synergies are likely especially in intact teams. Easy and obvious choices can be made on the spot. Follow-up and expectations for next steps can be described with immediate feedback from the group and agreement. An initial expectation for model implementation is achieved and commitment for support made.

These reviews are amazing activities to watch and typically take a few hours. In a sense they are organizational effectiveness reviews and deep alignments. While some things may become projects there is no detailed action planning done in the session. The awareness models and other artifacts can be used for broader communication to teams who are impacted by the paradoxes and changes suggested with an opportunity for further alignment and agreement.

The outcomes of the renewal phase are described by the paradox of intention and action. The intention is set in the final review as a close approximation that may be modified as others are included, and feedback is generated. The first step after the sessions is to communicate to explain, gain feedback for modification, and build support. This is essentially a change intervention that started when the workshop was initially planned and will continue through implementation of actions and modified system stability.

The Intention and Action statements describe what is planned to be accomplished and the nature of who we want to be during that process. The models created in the workshop are easy to use for explanation and the same open approach should be used as additional feedback and engagement is solicited. The opportunity for continued practice of paradoxical awareness and value is immediate. Workshop participants should share what they learned, engage others, and leverage the entire process to achieve a closer approximation to their leadership and performance intentions.

In Paradoxical Inquiry® practice the process leads to what we want in a fashion that is affirming and encouraging while practical and relevant. It is not accusatory or judgmental. It results in a shared understanding of What Is and agreement on What We Want. It strengthens teams and transforms organizations through the synergy of thinking together, positive conflict, and shared reality.

Chapter Eleven Summary

· Paradoxical inquiry defined: Paradoxical inquiry is a process for revealing, describing, evaluating, and intervening in paradoxical conditions.

· There are two types of paradoxical meaning making tools; those directly described as paradox interventions and a much larger set based on a paradoxical premise.

· Most problem-solving tools are extensions of the Good/Bad paradigm and immediately interject judgements.

· Paradoxical Inquiry® is a form of whole group mediation.

· Paradoxical Inquiry® Phases - Reveal, Reimagine, Refine, and Renew

· Paradoxical Inquiry® leads to what we want in a fashion that is affirming and encouraging while practical and relevant.

Unity

Paradoxical Inquiry®

Paradox

Conflict And Opportunity

Dependencies

Individual And Team
Opinions And Perspectives
Reality And Options
What Is And What you Want

Outcomes

Realization And Renewal
Shared Direction

Chapter 12

Chopping Wood and Carrying Water, The Paradox of Practice

Before enlightenment, chop wood and carry water.
After enlightenment, chop wood and carry water.

How do you get good at something? You practice. When do you practice? Purposively in certain times and situations, and effortlessly all the time because it is all practice. This is not hard; we have been doing it long before we knew what it was. Yet, if we want things to be closer to our conscious realization and expression it is helpful to reinforce them through repetition, application, and conscious training.

As you learn you start to notice without trying. Your assumptions and attributions shift to include the new view. As the Zen Koan above implies, what is different after learning isn't particularly what you do. You still accomplish the tasks that you always have. The possibility is you start to see them differently. When you recognize conflict, you may remember that it is the pattern of a paradox. When you experience confusion and disagreement you may be less inclined to argue who is right. Possibly you are more patient with others and more confident. You might relax a little when you remember that perfect is not the answer, close enough and as good as it gets are the real goals.

If you have read this book, I imagine that you have already developed greater paradoxical recognition and awareness. It is a very sticky concept and as you practice, it reveals more layers of meaning and value that you can apply toward your intention. I have purposively used a mix of ancient wisdom and modern science in my explanations. It may well be that the things that have stood the test of time, have done that for a good reason. We are on the verge of greater understanding through our scientific discoveries in neuroscience and cognitive science and we may discover that we already knew.

As we consider the outcomes of our choices and judgements of good or bad compared to the application of our intention with the judgement of what I want and who I want to be, we can see a fundamental difference in the outcomes. The good and bad choices follow the proverb of the Farmer and His Son. Are things good or bad? It depends and over time, Maybe. Good and Bad are always situational, not absolute. They are judgements with precision that lack accuracy. In applying our intention, aligning with what we prefer with a situation, the answer is, Yes. It remains yes until we want a different Yes. Paradoxically with less judgement we have greater surety that our decisions accomplish our purpose in a constantly evolving approximation.

Wherever you go, there you are. We can easily change the scenery, and if we want to change the view, we must adopt a different lens. The lens of paradox is the lens of acceptance. The acceptance of situations, intentions, others, and ourselves. Why are these concepts so sticky? Because they are true. True and false are not the same as good and bad.

These judgements reflect the character of our intentions and the fidelity of the realities we create to the situations they describe. We can build patterns that make sense in the light or that hide in the dark. The deception might be purposive, the intent to deceive. It may also be an error in understanding driven by an unquestioned bias, and it can also just be a less specific approximation compared to ours.

You might think that this is all just parsing words, and it is. We live in a semantic reality based on concepts and constructs. It is the mechanism to think beyond instinct. The instinctual self is still there. It is our reliable constant source of protection, bodily function, and the continuation of the human species. We are also a conscious self. The other side of the coin that describes our unity of being. This aware self creates great advantage in cooperation with our older, deeper self. They may seem like two things, and they are really just two aspects of the same thing. The wonderous aspect of all of this is that our conscious self is not limited to inhabiting only our bodies. We are creators beyond mere survival with the power to express ourselves in any way we choose, and paradoxical thinking is a tool we can apply to help us do that.

Unity

Practice

Paradox

Study And Feedback

Dependencies

Episodic And Continuous
Work And Play
Purposive And Emergent
Consistent And Diverse

Outcomes

Expert And Effortless
Competence

Many years ago, when I was in graduate school, I studied problem solving and the development of expertise. The Paradoxical Awareness Model above is my understanding of the pattern to accomplish the transition from novice to expert. The core effort is practice. As I learn new concepts and methods, I apply them in practice and the cycle continues as I desire until I reach Mastery.

I know you have experienced this. We all have. It isn't particularly difficult. Remember that play is a core enabling process in this all. How did we become good at riding a bike, we played, we had fun, it became so natural that we didn't even think about it. We have all done this many times, in many domains from the mundane to the extraordinary, the basics of caring for ourselves to our most treasured forms of expression.

Practicing a means to see more broadly and focus more clearly is accomplished in exactly the same fashion. By reading this book, you have built a sufficient foundation for initial practice. Depending on where you were with your study of this concept before you read the book, you might be practicing more advanced application. It may also still not make much sense, and that is OK too. Do what makes sense to you and apply the ideas and methods that support and accelerate your intention. That is the path. What you want and who you want to be.

Let's look a little more closely at each of the paradoxes and dependencies. These are not particularly in a required order. The components are generally all continuous. The power that turns this on, is your intention. From there you build new mental models as you learn. The paradox of practice includes two types of learning: study, and feedback. We read, observe, ask others, and reflect to form our ideas. A wonderful paradox is that we feed our minds and it does all the work without our direct intervention for the most part. The second path of learning from practice is feedback. We see what works and what doesn't both for ourselves and others. We may have help from teachers and coaches (formal and informal), and we can do it by ourselves. The core thing we need to know is what the next step of approximate performance looks like. We can use a model, observations of someone we think does it well, and even trial and error, they all work.

An example of Episodic And Continuous would be a commitment to weight loss or better physical performance. We periodically do exercise and we become constantly aware of what we eat and our food choices. For paradoxical thinking we might practice using the Awareness Model like a puzzle and pay general attention when we recognize paradoxes. An easy way is to do a simple analysis of commercials and see the associations the marketers are making.

Work And Play are environments of opportunity. We generally are already there so let's take advantage of them. These will be where we continue to practice and the beneficiaries of our achievement. Be opportunistic within what feels comfortable and appropriate. This is the Purposive and Emergent part. Plan some things and take advantage of opportunities as they come up. No one needs to know you are doing this unless you want to include them. Eventually, I think you will find direct application in both worlds where you will want to share to help yourself and others find more success with important intentions.

Consistent And Diverse are the practice of Deep and Wide. Typically, we develop a core and work out from there. For paradoxical thinking awareness is a likely core and novel situations and conflicts provide the variability to expand your performance range. The identification and application in different environments can be Structured And Free Form. Think of this like playing a game with a lot of rules and playing another game that you just make up on the fly. There is a lot of potential to use paradox in structured brainstorming and even group games that you can make. You can also be very improvisational pairing up associations randomly and challenging yourself to see unities or picking unities and uncovering some underlying paradoxes.

Two more concepts to share. The first is that we have discussed essentially a single layer of complexity. That is really useful, and it naturally is much more complex. The complexity leads to the second concept, the paradox of Outcomes that includes Intended And Unintended results.

Since paradox is a fractal concept, complexity is built on simplicity. It isn't a different concept at each level it just encompasses a larger set of information in the pattern. The patterns are of course approximations such that we maintain a workable view of our realities. I think of this a bit like a general background with more detail as we focus. For example, look out the window. Maybe you see houses and cars and trees and maybe some people walking by. You have the full view your eyes provide and at the same time your mind is not filled with everything these things mean to you.

Unless you think about it you are not immediately aware of everything you know about plant biology, the shapes of the different types of leaves on the ground, the history of the neighborhood, the exact appearance of the streetlight, or the details of a face that is unfamiliar. You may see all of these, and unless movement or difference or some other attention getting aspect is going on, you just see a general outside. Now this is different if you look with intention, like trying to see if it looks like rain, or if there is a package on the porch, or if a guest is approaching for lunch. When you think about this, our approximate attention is an amazing thing. We are super-efficient and focused on what is important to us and what we want, and need, to know more about.

Think about any situation you find yourself in, watching TV, driving down the street, or in a class. All of these unity concepts have a myriad number of conceptual paradoxes that contribute patterns, and depending on our attention we see a few of them, and for those, just a limited amount of detail. When we create the Paradoxical Awareness Models we are arranging concepts in an easy to see and understand form. What does it really look like? We don't know. The good news is that our mind does this automatically and just realize that there is a lot more going on out there than we are aware of.

We do know enough about our observed realities to be useful. The Awareness Models are a nice summary approximation and if we need more information, we can add layers to focus more discreetly or open ourselves to a larger frame of reference to see more broadly. What is important to us is the standard for exploration. It reveals our intent even if we never thought about it. Doing this with others who are also familiar with a situation expands our awareness through social cognition to get an even better approximation of What Is.

The final area of consideration is intended and unintended results. The saying when you pull a string you never know what it is attached to is true. I'm sure you've had the experience of doing something expecting a specific result and getting that plus something else. This works to our benefit and against it. You meet a random person at a party, you are pleasant and engaging and they think, "I wonder if they would be interested in the job I have open?" You go out to work in the yard and use a spray to kill weeds and you end up with a dead patch of grass. We are always in a complex system, our environments, social and individual contexts, and all of the other layers of meaning that describe What Is. This is a primary reason to use nudges for change instead of immediate large-scale approaches. Even if you have grand plans go with approximate steps.

Summary Chapter Twelve

· Practice is how you get good at something.

· You practice purposively in certain times and situations, and effortlessly all the time because it is all practice.

· Work and Play are the core environments for practice.

· Good and bad choices follow the proverb of the Farmer and His Son. Maybe. In applying our intention, aligning with what we prefer with a situation, the answer is, Yes.

· Our mental models/patterns are approximations such that we maintain a workable view of our realities.

· We are always in a complex system, our environments, social and individual contexts, and all the other layers of meaning that describe What Is

Unity
Practice

Paradox
Study And Feedback

Dependencies
Episodic And Continuous
Work And Play
Purposive And Emergent
Consistent And Diverse

Outcomes
Expert And Effortless
Competence

Essential Bibliography and a Few Favorite Works

Brooks, D. 2012. *The social animal.* New York: Random House.

Cooperrider, D.A. and Whitney, D. 2005. *Appreciative inquiry: a positive revolution in change.* San Francisco: Berrett-Koehler.

Dyer, W. 2008. *Living the wisdom of the Tao.* Carlsbad, CA: Hay House.

Farson, R. 1996. *Management of the absurd.* New York: Touchstone.

Flesher, J. 2021. Leadership from below; paradoxes of submarine leadership. Niantic, CT: Wisdom Mates Press.

Kahneman, D. 2011. *Thinking, fast and slow.* New York: Farrar, Straus, and Giroux.

Musashi, M. and Groff, D. (Translator). 2016. *The five rings: Miyamoto Musashi's art of strategy.* New York: Chartwell.

Russell, B., 1972. *The history of western philosophy.* New York: Simon & Schuster.

Suzuki, S. 2020. *Zen mind, Beginner's mind: informal talks on Zen meditation and practice, 50th anniversary edition.* Boulder, CO: Shambhala Publications.

Smith, W., Lewis, M., Jazabkowski, P, and Langley, A. (Editors). 2017. *Oxford handbook of organizational paradox.* New York: Oxford University Press.

Wegner, D. 2018. *The illusion of conscious will.* Cambridge, MA: MIT Press.

About the Author

Jeff Flesher is originally from Terre Haute, Indiana. He served in the United States Navy in the Submarine Service.

He completed a B.S. degree in History at the University of the State of New York, an M.S. in Technology Education at Eastern Illinois University, and a Ph.D. at the University of Illinois at Urbana-Champaign. His research area was problem-solving and the development of expertise. He also completed a Professional Certificate in Mediation at Cornell University.

Dr. Flesher has been a Professor at the University of Illinois at Urbana-Champaign, Southern Illinois University Carbondale, Iowa State University, and Roosevelt University.

Jeff led Learning and Organization Development groups at Commonwealth Edison, Abbott Laboratories, Biomet Inc., and Underwriters Laboratories. He is the owner of Wisdom Mates, LLC. He is also the author of Leadership From Below; Paradoxes of Submarine Leadership. Jeff and Bonnie have two daughters and five grandchildren and live in Niantic, CT.

Connections and Opportunities for Use

The information and concepts described in this work are the sole products of the author Jeffrey Flesher. These may be cited with attribution. The Paradoxical Inquiry Awareness Model$^{\copyright}$ or Paradox Awareness Model$^{\copyright}$ may be used with attribution for non-commercial purposes including research intended for publication and further debate and expansion of paradox related research. Paradoxical Inquiry$^{\circledR}$ is a United States registered Trademark and is not to be used for any commercial purpose without consent of the author with the exception of certified and licensed individuals and organizations.

For information on paradox inquiry sessions, speaking engagements, licensing and certification in Paradoxical Inquiry:

ParadoxUniversity.com
Paradoxicalinquiry.com
WisdomMates.com
WisdommatesLLC@gmail.com

To follow Jeff on social media:
LinkedIn.com - www.linkedin.com/in/jeff-flesher-43622a3

To everything there is a season,
and a time to every purpose under the heaven:
A time to be born, and a time to die;
a time to plant, and a time to pluck up that
which is planted;
A time to kill, and a time to heal;
a time to break down, and a time to build up;
A time to weep, and a time to laugh;
A time to mourn, and a time to dance;
A time to cast away stones, and a time to gather
stones together;
A time to embrace, and a time to refrain from
embracing;
A time to get, and a time to lose;
A time to keep, and a time to cast away;
A time to rend, and a time to sew;
A time to keep silence, and a time to speak;
A time to love, and a time to hate;
a time of war, and a time of peace.

Ecclesiastes 3:1-8

New King James Version
https://biblehub.com/

www.ingramcontent.com/pod-product-compliance
Lightning Source LLC
Chambersburg PA
CBHW052039150726
48002CB00002B/669